Tor & Darknet in the Art of Anonymity
by Raffaele De Rosa

You want what you want.
Invisibility. Anonymity. Ghost protocol.
You've taken the red pill and have seen
the truth, and you don't like it. I don't
blame you. I didn't like it either. But
what I thought I knew about Tor and
other incognito tools was only a drop in
the ocean next to what's really out there.
Stuff you don't find on many tech forums.They're whispered in private, of course,
but it's all invisible to you. Until now.
Which brings us to you and I, or rather
what I can do for you. It's amazing what
a guy can learn in a decade when he
rolls his sleeves up and gets his hands
dirty. Private hacker forums. Usenet.
Freenet. I scoured them all for years and
what I've learned isn't anywhere else on
Amazon.
Equally amazing is what you can learn
for a few dollars in a weekend's worthof reading. That's me, and soon to be
you. Where you will be by Monday is
where I am now, only without the years
of mistakes. Mistakes I made using
Freenet, Tails, PGP. You name it, I did it.
And boy did I make BIG ONES.
Mistakes you'll avoid because after you
read this guide, you'll know more than
85% of the Tor users out there, and know
more about anonymity than most Federal
agents. Yes, even the so-called
superhackers at the NSA.
If you don't come away satisfied, returnit for a full refund.
But I know you won't. Because once
you've taken the red pill, there ain't no
going back. You can't unlearn what

you've learned, unsee what you've seen,
and you'll want more. Much, much more.
First off, we're not sticking with the
basics here. If all you want is Tor for
Dummies, look elsewhere. Where we're
going is dangerous territory. It's shark
territory when you get right down to it.
But not to worry. We've got sharkrepellant and everything you need to surf
safe. You'll reap benefits you've only
dreamed of and by the time we're done,
you'll have gained NSA-level anonymity
skills with a counter-surveillance
mindset that rivals anything Anonymous
or those goons at the NSA can counter
with.
Speaking of which, they won't have a
clue as to how to find you.
Secondly, for a few dollars you will
know every exploit those superhackerslike to wield against Tor users and more:
How to avoid NSA tracking. Bitcoin
anonymity (real anonymity), Opsec
advice and Darknet markets and
Darkcoins and, well, it's a long list
frankly, but by the time you're done
you'll be a Darknet artist when it comes
to marketplaces and buying things
incognito.
Third, we'll go over many techniques
used by the CIA and FBI to entrap users.
False confessions. Clickbait. Tor
honeypots. It's all the same. You'll learnthe same techniques used to catch
terrorists, hackers and the group
Anonymous and couriers for Reloaded.
Baits and Lures and how to spot an LEA
agent from a mile away. I break it all
down into simple steps that you can
understand. A few dollars for this info
will save you a LIFETIME of grief. No,
you won't find it on Reddit or Ars
Technica or Wired. If you're mulling this
over, don't. You need this now, not when
you're framed for something you didn't
do.Fourth... reading the dangerous material
herein requires you take ACTION. The
Feds take action. Identity thieves take

action. Hackers take action. Will you?
Make no mistake - This is not a mere
guide. It is a mindset. It's professional
level stuff meant to keep you and your
family safe for a decade out, going far
beyond apps and proxies. And it's all
yours if you do two simple things: You
read, then act. Simple. Because you
know what they say: Knowledge is
power.No, strike that. Knowledge is potential
power. Your power. But only if you act.
Fifth... I update this book every month.
New browser exploit in the wild? I
update it here. New technique for
uncloaking Tor users? You'll read it here
first. We all know how Truecrypt is Not
Safe Anymore, but that's only the
beginning.
Besides, freedom isn't free.
Lastly... The scene from Jurassic Parkwith Dennis Nedry, I believe, is a nice
frightful analogy to what happens if you
don't take your security seriously. We
see poor Dennis try to get his jeep out of
the muck in the middle of a tropical
storm. Lightning unzips the sky and the
rain pours. The thunder rolls. A
dilophisaur bounds upon him, beautiful,
yet painted across his ugly mug is a
deadly curiosity as it sniffs the air and
cocks it's head at Nedry - moments
before spraying his chubby eyes with
poison. Blinded, he staggers back to the
safety of the jeep, wailing and gnashingteeth, only to discover a visual horror to
his right: he's left the passenger-side
door ajar - wide enough to let Mr.
Curious in for a juicy evening meal -
which it savors with a row of sharp
teeth.

The point is this: Don't be Dennis Nedry.
There are far bigger creatures who'd like
nothing better than to split your life (and
family) wide open if for no other reason
than THEY CAN, such is the nature of
the elite.Unless, of course, you tame them...

Not bloody likely.Is Tor Safe?
That seems to be the question,
alright. And to that, well, it really
depends on whom you ask, because there
are always wolves in sheep's clothing
out there who stand to gain from your
ignorance. Many say no. A few say yes.
The media, for all their expertise in
things political and social, come up
woefully lacking when something ascomplex as Tor is discussed.
Case in point: Gizmodo reported that
in December, 2014, a group of hackers
managed to compromise enough Tor
relays to decloak Tor users. If you're just
hearing this for the first time, part of
what makes Tor anonymous is that it
relays your data from one node to
another. It was believed that if they
compromised enough of them, then they
could track individual users on the Tor
network and reveal their real life
identities. Kind of like how the agents inThe Matrix find those who've been
unplugged.
Anyway as luck would have it, it
turned out to be kiddie script-hackers
with too much time on their hands who
simply wanted a new target to hack.
Who knows why. Could be that they'd
toyed with the Playstation Network and
Xbox users long enough and simply
wanted a curious peak here and there.
These were not superhacker-level NSA
members, either.But as is usually the case with the
media, this attack attracted the attention
of a few bloggers and tech journalists
unsympathetic to Tor and frankly,
ignorant of what really constitutes a
threat. The Tor devs commented on it,
too:
"This looks like a regular attempt
at a Sybil attack: the attackers have
signed up many new relays in hopes of
becoming a large fraction of the
network. But even though they are
running thousands of new relays, theirrelays currently make up less than 1%

of the Tor network by capacity. We are working now to remove these relays from the network before they become a threat, and we don't expect any anonymity or performance effects based on what we've seen so far."

What those conspiracy bloggers failed to report was that any decentralized network like Tor is a prime target for attacks such as the above. But to truly stand a chance at punching a hole through this matrix,hackers would need Tor to implicitly trust every new node that comes online.

That doesn't happen.

It also takes time for fresh relays to gather traffic - some as long as sixty days or more and the likelihood of being reported is rather high since the IP addresses are out in the open - which only speeds up malicious reporting. The real danger, and has been since inception, is scaring Tor users to less secure methods of communication. That's what the NSA wants. The CIA alreadydoes this in foreign countries. Now the NSA is following their lead.The REAL Risk of Using Tor

I list them here before we dive deep into enemy territory so you'll know what to avoid before installation, and maybe get an "a-ha!" moment in subsequent chapters. As you read, remember that having Javascript on is really only a drop in the ocean next to what is possible for an enemy to kill your anonymity.Javascript

It's widely known that leaving Javascript on is bad for a Tor user. Ninety-five percent of us know this, but the mistakes of the 5% get blown out of proportion and thrown into the face of the rest of us. Worse, many websites now run so many scripts that it seems as though they hate Tor users.

One site required over a dozen. Without it, the page was/is/will be pretty much gimped. Sometimes not evenreadable. You can imagine what might

happen if you were using Tor and
decided to visit that site if it was set up
to lure users into a honeypot.
I remember one researcher claimed
that "81% of Tor users can be de-
anonymised."
Bull.
That 81% figure came about because
the targeted users knew little about the
NoScript browser add-on, and likelymixed Tor usage with their daily open
net usage, providing ample data for a
correlation attack. But that was just the
icing on the cake. They left personal
details *everywhere* - using the same
usernames and passes they do elsewhere
on the open net. Bragging about their
favorite Netflix movies. Talking about
local events (Jazzfest in New Orleans!).
The weather (Hurricane in the French
Quarter!). You get the idea.
Volunteering as an Exit NodeAnother doozy, though not quite the
granddaddy of all risks, but still risky.
On the plus side, you as a valiant
believer in anonymity graciously
provide bandwidth and an "exit pipe" to
the rest of the Tor users (hopefully none
of whom you know) so that they may
pass their encrypted traffic through your
node. Generous? Certainly. Wise? If you
live in the States... hale no as my Uncle
Frick in Texas used to say.
It isn't that it is illegal per se to do
so. On the contrary, but what passesthrough your node can land you in hot
water if you live in a police state. All
exiting traffic from your node (i.e. other
people's traffic) is tied to your IP
address and as others have found, you
put yourself at risk by what others on the
other side of the planet do with your
node.
Lots of new Tor users fire up
BitTorrent configured for Tor and suck
down all the bandwidth. It makes for a
very miserable Tor experience for other
users. You may get served with acopyright violation notice (or sued), or

perhaps raided if child porn flows out of your pipes. Think carefully and do your research before taking on such a risky charge, lest your computer be seized and your reputation ruined.

Running an Exit Relay From Home

Running it from home is even worse then using cloud storage, and is infinitely dangerous in the USA and UK. If the law for whatever reason has an interest in your Tor traffic, your PC might beseized, yes, but that's only the start. In the UK, there is no 5th amendment protection against self-incrimination. A crusty old judge can give you two years just for not forking over the encryption keys (which if they had, they would not have bothered raiding at 6AM).

Use a host instead that supports Tor. There is Sealandhosting.org, for one. They accept Bitcoins and do not require any personal info, only an email. They offer Socks, Dedicated Servers, Tor Hosting and VPS as well as Domains. We'll get into the nitty details later, but these are the Rules I've set for myself:

- Refrain from routing normal traffic through it
- Never do anything illegal (more later as it's a grey area)
- Never put sensitive files on it (financial info, love notes, court docs)
- Be as transparent as possible that I'm running an exit
- If I get complaints from The OldeISP (or university), I use this template.

Intelligence Agencies

They've declared war on Tor and its stealth capabilities, no doubt about it. And though they will fight tooth and nail to convince you it is for your own good, really what it all comes down to isn't so much national security as it is national control: Control over you in that they know not what you're doing on Tor, nor why. They don't like that.

It's quite galactically pompous of

them to spend so much money and waste
so much time chasing you simply
because they don't like you or your
actions not being easily identifiable.
As you probably know, it's more
costly to go after a high-value target. But
they do not know if you are a high-value
target or merely low-hanging fruit. As
we've seen in the case of bored Harvardstudents, anyone can get into serious
trouble if they go into Tor blind as a bat.
Even Eric Holder has publicly
pointed out that Tor users are labeled as
"non-US persons" until identified as
citizens. It's beyond pompous. It's
criminal and unconstitutional. It sounds
as if they view ALL Tor users as high-
value targets.

And by the time you are identified as
such, they have acquired enough power
to strip you as well as millions of othercitizens of their rights to privacy and
protection under the Fourth Amendment
of the Constitution.
They do this using two methods:
The Quantum and FoxAcid System
More on how to defeat this later, but
here is the gist of it:
- Both systems depend on secret
arrangements made with telcos- Both involve lulling the user into a
false sense of security
- Neither system can make changes
to a LiveCD (Tails)
- Both can be defeated by adhering
to consistent security habits.
Defeating this requires a mindset of
diligence. DO NOT procrastinate.
Decide ahead of time to avoid risky
behavior. We'll get to them all. A good,
security mindset takes time and effortand commitment to develop but should
be nurtured from the very beginning,
which is why the RISKS are placed up
front, ahead of even the installation
chapter. Things tend to drag in the
middle of a book like this, and are often
forgotten.

Speaking of risk... if you wonder
what truly keeps me up at night, it's this:
What do other nations tell high-level
CEOs and Intelligence agencies (Hong
Kong, for instance)?If the only thing I can trust is my
dusty old 486 in my attic with Ultima 7
still installed atop my 28.8k dialup
modem, then it's safe to assume every
commercial entity is jeopardized by the
NSA. And if that's true, if the NSA has to
jump hoops to spy on us, how easy is it
to infiltrate American-owned systems
overseas with our data on those
systems?
To that, if no corporation can keep
their private info under wraps, then
eventually the endgame may evolve intoa Skynet grid similar to the Soviet-era
East/West block in which CEOs have to
choose east or west. But that's like trying
to decide whether you want to be eaten
by a grizzly bear or a lion.
So then, you now know the real
risks. The main ones, anyway.
Every one of these risks can be
minimized or outright defeated using
knowledge that is in this book. The sad
part is that most readers will forget
roughly 80% of what they read. Thosewho take action will retain that 80%
because they are making what they've
read a reality: Making brilliant
chesslike countermoves when the NSA
threatens your Queen. If you do not take
action ,but merely sit there like a frog in
a slowly boiling pot of water, not only
will you perish but your future
generations will as well. Alright then.
Enough of the risks. Let's get to it.Tor Step-by-Step Guide
Now let's answer what Tor is and
what it does and what it cannot do.
You've no doubt heard it is some kind of
hacker's tool, and you'd be right, but only
from the perspective that a powerful tool
like Tor can be used for just about
anything. In fact anything can be bought
(except maybe voluptuous blondes in red

dresses) anonymously... as long as you're
cautious about it.Before you knock Tor, remember that
it is not about buying drugs or porn or
exotic white tiger cubs. It's about
anonymous communication and privacy -
with the main function being to grant you
anonymity by routing your browsing
session from one Tor relay to another--
masking your IP address such that
websites cannot know your real
location.
This allows you to:- Access blocked websites
(Facebook if you are in China)
- Access .onion sites that are
unreachable via the open internet
- Threaten the president with a pie-
to-the-face...and no Secret Service visit!
It does all of this by a process called
onion routing.
What is onion routing?
Think of it as a multi-point-to-point
proxy matrix. Unlike peer to peerapplications like BitTorrent or eMule
which expose your IP to everyone, Tor
uses a series of intermediary nodes (and
thus, IPs) that encrypt your data all along
the network chain. At the endpoint, your
data is decrypted by an exit node so that
no one can pinpoint your location or tell
which file came from which computer.
Due to this anonymizing process, you are
anonymous on account of the packed
"onion layers" that hide your true IP
address.
It is even possible to build a sitesuch that only Tor users can access it.
Also called "Onion Sites," though
technically challenging, you don't need a
Ph.D in computer science to build one.
Or even a Bachelor's degree. These
Onion sites are unaccessible by anyone
using the regular web and regular, non-
Tor Firefox.
We'll delve deeper into that later, as
well as construct a fortress of doom that
nothing can penetrate.Installation
Installing Tor is dirt simple. You can

download it here.
If your ISP blocks you from the Tor
site, do this:
- Shoot an email to Tor. Tell them the
situation. You can get an automated
message sent back to you with the Tor
installation package.- Go to Google. Do a search for any
cached websites, including Tor, that
might have the install package to
download. Many tech sites may just have
it in the event of all-out nuclear war.
- Visit rt.torproject.org and ask them
to mirror it.
- Get a friend to email you the Tor
installation. Ask for Tails, too.
- VERIFY the signature if you obtain
it elsewhere other than from the mainTor site, but for the love of all that is
sacred and holy, Threepwood, verify it
even if your friend hand-delivers it. I've
gotten viruses in the past from friend's
sharing what they thought were "clean"
apps.
Now then. Choose Windows, Linux
or the Mac version and know that your
default Firefox install will not be
overwritten unless you want it to. Both
use Firefox but Tor is a completely
separate deal. You'll notice it has the
same functions as Firefox: Tabs.Bookmarks. Search box. Menus. It's all
here... except your favorite add-ons.
And on that point, you might be
tempted to install your favorites. Don't
give in to that temptation. Multiple add-
ons that do nothing for your anonymity
might assist someone in locating you
over Tor by what is known as "Browser
fingerprinting."After installation, you should see the
green welcome screen below:Now you've got some choices. One
is to volunteer your bandwidth, which
makes it easier for other Tor users but
comes with risk. It is explained in-depth
by Tor developers here. I'd recommend
reading it if you are new to anonymity
tools.
After Tor is installed, every page

you visit with the Tor Browser will be
routed anonymously through the Tor
network. There is however an important
detail you need to know concerningsecurity, and that is that your Tor settings
are merely reasonable starting points.
They are not optimal. We're still at the
infancy stage and quite frankly, optimal
as Tor knows optimal is largely
dependent on hardware (network, CPU,
RAM, VM, VPN), and so each person's
setup will be different.What Tor Cannot Do
Now for what Tor cannot do, or at
least cannot do very well. In the future
this may change so don't fall on your
sword just yet.
1.) Tor cannot protect you from
attachments.
This is not limited to executables,
but anything that can be run via code.
This means Flash videos as well asRealPlayer and Quicktime. Those babies
can be configured to send your real IP
address to an adversary. Not good. So
never run any executable or app unless
you trust the source. If at all possible, go
open-source. This also goes for any
encryption scheme which you MUST use
if you're going to use Tor. It is NOT an
option. Some say it is but that's like
saying learning Thai is optional if you're
going to live in Bangkok. You won't get
far that way.
2.) Tor cannot run torrents well.Old news, right? Thousands still do
this. Better safe than sorry, they claim.
Only problem is... they are safe and
everyone else is sorry. Tor cannot do
P2P apps like Emule and Limewire
without making everyone else's Tor
experience miserable. It simply sucks
down too much bandwidth. In addition to
some exit nodes blocking such traffic by
default, it's been proven that an IP
address can be found by using torrents
over Tor. eMule, too, uses UDP and
since Tor supports TCP protocol, youcan draw your own conclusions about
what that does to your anonymity.

True, you may be spared a copyright lawsuit since the RIAA likely won't go through all that trouble in trying to get your IP, but please spare other Tor users the madness of 1998 modem speeds. A VPN is a much better choice. There are a few good ones out there.

3.) Tor cannot cloak your identity if you are tossing your real email around like Mardi Gras beads. If you give yourtrue email on websites while using Tor, consider your anonymity compromised. Your virtual identity must never match up with your real-life identity. Ever. Those who ignore this rule get hacked, robbed, arrested, or mauled by capped gremlins. Much more on this later.

Tor Apps & Anti-Fingerprinting Tools

A few applications make Tor less of a headache, but they are not particularlywell suited for desktop users unless you're doing some kind of emulation. But with everyone using mobile these days, some of these have benefited me in ways I never thought possible. Be sure and read the comments in the Play Store since updates tend to break things.

Orbot: Proxy with Tor

Tor for Android, check it out here.It is a proxy app that runs similar to the desktop app and encrypts your net traffic and protects you from surveillance and fortifies you against traffic analysis. You can use Orbot withTwitter, DuckDuckGo or any app with a proxy feature. I've used this for a long time now and have gotten used to it. Perhaps it is time to try something else.

Invisibox - Privacy Made EasyJust plug the InvizBox into your existing router / modem. A new "InvizBox" wifi hotspot will appear. Connect to the new hotspot and follow the one time configuration set up and you're ready to go. All devices that you connect to the InvizBox wifi will route their traffic over the Tor Network.

Text SecureThis app encrypts every message on your mobile phone and is simple to

learn. Better still, in the event you leave
your phone at Marble Slab (Marble Flab
to the Mrs.), rest assured your privacy is
safe due to encryption. It's also open-
source. Far too many apps aren't, and
thus cannot be peer-reviewed by, well,anyone, unlike some proprietary apps
like those offered by SecurStar (i.e.
Drivecrypt, Phonecrypt).
Red Phone
This app secures every call withend-to-end encryption, allowing you
privacy and peace of mind. It uses WiFi
and offers neat upgrades if both callers
have RedPhone installed.
It's not for everyone. Though it's not
as expensive as say, TrustCall, there are
convenience issues like lengthy
connection times and dropped calls
(ever Skype someone from Manila?) so
it's not going to be as quick and dirty as
Jason Bourne does it.
But the pluses outweigh the minuses.I especially love the two-word
passphrase as a security feature: If you
fear Agent Boris is dead and has been
killed by Agent Doris (who now has his
phone), you can request she speak the
second passphrase. Simple yet effective.
Google and TorWhat does Google think of Tor?
Quite honestly I suspect they try not to.
They probably don't hate it like the
NSA does, but they know that if every
Google user used Tor on a daily basis,
much of their ad targeting system would,shall we say, begin firing blanks.
Imagine if a thirteen year old boy
received ads for Cialis, or an eighty-
year old woman named Bertha began to
see ads for Trojan coupons, or... well
you get the idea.
They don't mind donating funds,
either, since this allows a future stake in
the technology (sort of). To that, they've
not only donated to Tor, but to Freenet as
well and even Mars rover technology.
All kinds of crazy things. They never
know which technology is going torocket into orbit a week or year from
now so they throw money around like

Scrooge on Christmas morning.

Captchas

At times you'll be using Tor and find that Google spits this requirement out in order to prove you're human. This, on account of their massive analyses on search queries, is what drives some Tor users to think Google has it out for them. However, Google has to put up withlots of spammers and general thievery; bots hammering the servers with tons of queries in short amounts of time that put undue strain on the servers can be one thing, but it can also happen if your employer uses proxies - many employees working for the same company that uses one of these can set off a red flag.

When your Tor circuit switches to a new one, usually it solves itself. There are other search engines like DuckDuckGo you can use, however.You may find websites do the same thing. Again, this is on account of so many exit nodes (all of which are publicly visible to any website admin), slamming the website with traffic such that the hammering behavior resemble those of a bot, the kind Russian and Chinese outfits like to use.

Tor developers have some interesting things as well on this topic. https://www.torproject.org/docs/faq.hSpiderOak

Normally I warn against using Cloud Service for anything you want private. SpiderOak one exception, with some reservation. It's a decent enough alternative to DropBox as it is coded with "Zero Knowledge" (so say the developer) and when you install it, a set of encryption keys is created client-side. When you upload data to SpiderOak servers, they're encrypted on *your*computer and *then* uploaded. Again, according to the developers.

They claim that even if a subpoena requires subscriber data, they could not deliver since only you have the keys.

Not bad, but I still would not upload
anything unencrypted. A container file,
for instance.
The other downside is that it is
centralized. Centralization means a
single-point-of-failure. As well your
data can be deleted by them at any time
(true with any online service really).
Remember that between you and a judge,they will always side with the judge.Tails
Ever heard of a "live system"?
Neither had I until Tails burst on the
scene. Tails allows you to use Tor and
avoid tracking and censorship and in just
about any location you could want. It
houses its own operating system and is
designed for those on the go.You can run it via USB stick, SD or
even a DVD. Pretty handy as this makes
it resistant to viruses. It's also beneficial
if you don't want your hard drive to
leave remnants of your browsing
session. The best part is that it's free and
based on Linux annnd comes with chat
client, email, office, and browser.
The downside to using a DVD is that
you must burn it again each time you
update Tails. Not very convenient. So
let's install it to USB stick instead.1.) Download tails installer here.
You must first install it somewhere, like
a DVD, and THEN clone it the USB
stick or SD card.
2.) Click Applications --> Tails -->
Tails install to begin the installation.
3.) Choose Clone & Install to install
to SD card or USB Memory Stick
4.) Plug in your device, then scan for
the device in the Target-Device dropdown menu. You'll get a warning about it
overwriting anything on the device,
blah-blah. Choose yes and confirm
install.
Tails Limitations
Neither Tails nor Tor encrypt your
docs automatically. You must use GnuPG
or LUKS for that (included), bearing in
mind that some docs like Word or
Atlantis may have your registration info

within the document itself (In 2013,Amazon self-publishers discovered pen names could sometimes be revealed by looking at the code of the above apps and finding out the real identity of authors. Ouch.)

Personally I use fake info when "registering" any app I will use in conjunction with Tor or Tails.

Other noteworthy stuff:

- Document metadata is not wiped with Tails- Tails does not hide the fact you're using it from your ISP (unless you use Tor bridges). They cannot see what you're doing on Tor, true enough, but they know you're using it.

- Tails is blind to human error. Try not to use the same Tails session to begin two different projects. Use separate sessions. Isolating both identities in this way contributes to strong anonymity for your sessions.

Chrome

Firefox is hardly the only way to slay a dragon. There's also Chrome. Yes, it's Google, and yes Google has strayed far from it's "Do No Evil" motto, but like everything else in life, luck favors the prepared. You just have to have the right sword. The right armor. The right lockpicks. The preparations (reagents) are as follows:

I. Install the ScriptNo extension. It isto chrome what a mouse is for a PC, at least as far as precision aiming goes. It offers excellent control, too, even allowing you to fine-tune the browser in ways that NoScript for Firefox cannot. If you find it too difficult, ScriptSafe is another option. I've used both and came away very satisfied, though like everything else on the internet, YMMV.

II. FlashControl is a nice alternative to Firefox. In the event you don't see it in the Google Play Store, just search for "Flash Block" and it should come up(Google has a habit of removing apps

that aren't updated every Thursday under
a Full Moon).
III. Adblock. This one is just
insanely good at repelling all kinds of
malware.
IV. User-agent Switcher for Chrome.
Install it. Never leave home (0.0.0.0)
without it. It spoofs and mimics user-
agent strings. You can set yours to look
like Internet Explorer. This will fool a
lot of malware payloads into thinkingyou really are browsing with IE and not
Firefox or Chrome, thus firing blanks at
you.
It might have saved Blake Benthall,
26 year old operator of Silk Road 2.0,
from getting raided by the FBI (among a
dozen other drug outfits). This was
accomplished over the span of many
months since they had to get control of
many relays, and if you have control of
relays, you can use sophisticated traffic
analysis to study patterns in IP addresses
and match behavior and browser settingswith those addresses. Recall that any
federal prosecutor will always try to tie
an IP address to an actual person where
felonies are concerned.
Let me repeat: An IP address is
considered an identity for the purposes
of prosecution. We're all a number to
them, regardless. Those of you with
student loans know this perhaps more
than anyone else. This will change as
time goes on of course - as Tor
competitors like Freenet and other apps
evolve to offer what Tor cannot. IvanPustogarov goes into much more detail
here on this but suffice to say the FBI did
their homework and when all was said
and done, had more resources on
identifying lazy users than a typical VPN
would. /endgame
V. CanvasBlocker - Annnnd another
great plugin for Firefox. This baby
prevents sites from using Javascript
<canvas> API to fingerprint users. You
can block it on every site or be

discriminant and block only a few sites.
Up to you. The biggest thing for me isthat it doesn't break websites. More info
here but in case you can't be bothered,
here's the gist:
The different block modes are:
</canvas></canvas></canvas>
- block readout API: All websites
not on the white list or black list can
use the <canvas> API to display
something on the page, but the readout
API is not allowed to return values to
the website.
- fake readout API: CanvasBlocker's default setting, and my
favorite! All websites not on the white
list or black list can use the <canvas>
API to display something on the page,
but the readout API is forced to return
a new random value each time it is
called.
- ask for readout API permission:
All websites not on the white list or
black list can use the <canvas> API to
display something on the page, but the
user will be asked if the website should
be allowed to use the readout API each
time it is called.- block everything: Ignore all lists
and block the <canvas> API on all
websites.
- allow only white list: Only
websites in the white list are allowed to
use the <canvas> API.
- ask for permission: If a website is
not listed on the white list or black list,
the user will be asked if the website
should be allowed to use the <canvas>
API each time it is called.
- block only black list: Block the
<canvas> API only for websites on the
black list.- allow everything: Ignore all lists
and allow the <canvas> API on all
websites.
As you can see, it's powerful stuff.
Deadly Firefox Options
Firefox
You might be tempted to enable

"Check for counterfeit websites" in
Firefox. Don't do this as it will relay
sites you regularly visit to Google'sservers. Google's "predictive text-
search" is also bad as it relays
keystrokes to Google as well. To change
it you have to do it manually by going
into about:config in the address bar.
That said, let's look at some other
privacy settings you might want to know
about.
Javascript - Avoid like the plague.
You may notice it is turned on by default
under the Firefox options tab, though.
The reason is spelled out here by the Tor
Developer Team:We configure NoScript to allow
JavaScript by default in Tor Browser
because many websites will not work
with JavaScript disabled. Most users
would give up on Tor entirely if a
website they want to use requires
JavaScript, because they would not
know how to allow a website to use
JavaScript (or that enabling JavaScript
might make a website work).
There's a tradeoff here. On the one
hand, we should leave JavaScript
enabled by default so websites work theway users expect. On the other hand,
we should disable JavaScript by default
to better protect against browser
vulnerabilities (not just a theoretical
concern!). But there's a third issue:
websites can easily determine whether
you have allowed JavaScript for them,
and if you disable JavaScript by default
but then allow a few websites to run
scripts (the way most people use
NoScript), then your choice of
whitelisted websites acts as a sort of
cookie that makes you recognizable
(and distinguishable), thus harmingyour anonymity.
Ghostery and Ghostrank - Not
deadly, just useless on Tor since Tor
disables tracking anyway. If you do use
it, either could possibly alter your
browser 'fingerprint', though not to the

extent of breaking anonymity. Ghostery
still blocks any tracking scripts
regardless if you're on Tor or not. But
use DuckDuckGo if you want to beef up
your anonymity.
Adblock - This could also changeyour fingerprint. Adblock plus has
"acceptable ads" enabled by default, and
there is also the scandals that Adblock
has been in over the years, one implying
that Google paid the Adblock CEO for
Google Ads to be shown.
Besides, the basic idea of the Tor
Browser Bundle is to use as few addons
as possible. They figure that TorButton,
NoScript, and HTTPS Everywhere is
sufficient to preserve anonymity without
the added risk of additional addons. Or
um... drama.The Panopticlick website may also
be useful to you.Whonix & Tor
If you're paranoid that using Tor
could get you into trouble (if you are
hosting a Hidden Service), you might
want to look into Whonix before running
anything. Many power users who use Tor
daily like the tighter security it offers.
This is not to say that it is better than
Tails by default. Both tools offer
strengths and weaknesses meant for
different purposes, and you may find oneis better than the other for your personal
situation.
Like Tails, Whonix is built with
anonymity and security in mind. It's also
based off of Debian/Linux, so it's a good
synergy where anonymity is concerned.
This synergy grants anonymity by routing
everything through Tor. The advantages
are that DNS leaks are next to
impossible and malware cannot reveal
your IP address. In fact, the only
connections possible are routed through
Tor via the Whonix-Gateway.The question you may be wondering
is: how much security is too much
security? What's overkill and what isn't?Well, you should ask how far will
you fall if caught, and how much time
are you willing to invest in reading to

prevent it. Tails is easier to grasp, and if
you do not expect attacks from sites you
visit then by all means use Tails.
If you live in North Korea or China
then there is a possibility of hard labor
hammering worthless rocks if they see
any Tor activity coming from your
location that correlates to "things they
don't like" activity... or anything else in
the case of NK that offers hope. Guiltyuntil proven innocent.
So if the above applies to you, use
Whonix as it offers more security.
From Whonix.org:A few notable features of Whonix
that make it more secure:
Anonymous Publishing/Anti-
Censorship
Anonymous E-Mail w/Thunderbirdor TorBirdy
Add proxy behind Tor (user -> Tor -
> proxy)
Chat anonymously.
IP/DNS protocol leak protection.
Hide that you are using Tor
Hide the fact you are using Whonix
Mixmaster over Tor
Secure And Distributed Time
Synchronization Mechanism
Security by Isolation
Send E-mail anonymously without
registration
Torify any appTorify Windows
Virtual Machine Images (VM)
VPN Support
Use Adobe Flash anonymously
Use Java/Javascript anonymously
The following is an example of a
moderately secure system:
- Host Whonix on a memory stick
with a flavor of Linux of your choice
- Use a VPN you trust (for privacy,not anonymity)
- Use Macchanger to spoof any mac
address every session (Whonix does not
hide your mac address from sites you
visit!). If Macchanger isn't to your liking,
give Technitium MAC Address Changer
a try.

- Avoid regular calls of non-Tor
WiFi tablets if using Cafe WiFi
- Know where every CCTV is
located in the area you plan to use TorMAC Addresses
We mentioned Mac addresses. Well
as technology would have it, your new
WiFi/Ethernet card has something that
can aid intelligence agencies in tracking
you. It's a 48-bit identifier burned-in by
the manufacturer. Sort of like an IMEI
for your phone. If by chance you were
not thinking clearly and bought your
computer with Tor in mind using a credit
card, you may later get targeted by an
FBI "NIT" that swipes your MACnumber. If that happens, you're toast.
More info here on this: Torsploit.
The way to defeat this is to have a
disposable MAC (the number, not the
Apple product). One that you bought
with cash with no security cams. That
way you can get rid of it in a flash or
swap it out.
They are also soft-configurable.
Believe it or not, Tails itself alters this
randomly with every session. With a
virtual machine, the FBI Nit may target aMAC number from the VirtualBox pool.
Not really an issue unless they happen to
raid your house and snag your system
simultaneously. So swapping this out on
a daily basis, as you've probably
guessed, can be quite a pain. It's mainly
for guys who run illegal markets. Guys
who are *always* in the crosshairs of
alphabet agencies.
But then, so can you. I've found it
pays to think of oneself higher than what
one is actually worth when traversing
dark nets. I.e. Thinking of yourself as ahigh value target. You'll
subconsciously program yourself to
research more, learn more - from
everything from bad security mistakes to
bad friendships to bad business
practices. To that, you don't have to be in
the top 5% of guys who've mastered
network security. Being in the top 25%

pool is more than enough to make The
Man get frustrated enough to look for his
flashy headlines elsewhere... for a low
hanging fruit named Neb who lives in
mama's basement, for instance. Whonix Bridges
If you live in a communist hellscape
where even mentioning Tor can get you
into trouble, using a Bridge with Whonix
can be quite literally a life saver.
What Bridges Are
Bridges are obfuscation tools to
cloak your Tor usage from a nosy ISP or
government who might see you are using
Tor, but not know what you are doing with it. To that end, Tor bridges are
alternative ways to enter the Tor
network. Some are private. Many are
public. Some are listed on the Tor
homepage. In a hostile environment you
can see the value in using it to your
advantage as it makes it much more
difficult for an ISP to know you're using
Tor.
What Bridges Are Not
While not especially unreliable, they
are certainly *less* reliable than regular Tor usage where performance goes. But
the tradeoff may be in your best interest.
Only you can decide if the performance
hit is warranted. Here's how to do it in
Whonix.
Bridges must be added manually
since there is no auto-install method for
Whonix, but it is not difficult. You
simply must enter them into the proper
directory:
/etc/tor/torrc. If you're using a graphical Whonix-
Gateway, then browse to:
Start Menu -> Applications ->
Settings -> /etc/tor/torrc.examples
To edit your torrc file (necessary for
bridge adding), browse to:
Start Menu -> Applications ->
Settings -> /etc/tor/torrc
Then add whatever bridge you
copied from the Tor bridges page (or a private one if you have it). Then restart
Tor for it to take effect. If you run into

trouble (and most likely will if it's your
first time) there are a few forums to help
you out.
Whonix Forum
Tor Reddit
Wilders Security Forum
QuoraTor and VPNs
There is a lot of confusion among
beginners when it comes to VPN
companies. They read one thing and see
something else in the media that
contradicts that one thing. The cold, hard
truth about VPN companies is that a few
want your patronage so badly that they're
likely to bury the fine print on their web
page where it is difficult to read.
Believe me, that's fine print that can getyou sent to the Big House if you're not
careful. It really is a minefield where
these companies are concerned.
For this reason, you need to decide
whether you want privacy or anonymity.
They are different beasts that require
different setups. And not every VPN user
uses Tor and not every Tor user uses a
VPN service, but it is advantageous to
combine two powerful tools; one that
affords privacy (the VPN) and one
anonymity (Tor). Like I said, two
different beasts.But for what it's worth, if you like
this combo then find a VPN that offers
128 bit encryption and that does not
store activity logs. That's the first rule
of business.
And here's the part where the fine
print comes in. Many VPN companies
claim they do not log a thing... but will
gladly offer your subscriber data on a
silver platter if a subpoena demands it.
Between Big Money and Your Freedom,
money always wins. They will not go tojail for you, ever. So do your due
diligence and research.
Obviously a VPN service is not
anonymous by default. Providers love to
tout that it is, but let's face it there is
nothing anonymous about using someone

else's line if you left a money trail
leading straight to your front door.
Enter Tor, slayer of gremlins and
we-know-what-is-better-for-you nanny
staters. Tor makes for an extra and
formidable layer of security in that thethieves will have to go an extra step to
steal something from you. Thieves come
in all flavors, from simple jewel thieves
to border guards who want to make you
as miserable as they are. So it is a good
idea to ensure all the holes in your Tor
installation are updated.
Updated applications are resistant to
malware attacks since it takes time to
find exploitable holes in the code. But...
if you do not update then it does not
matter which VPN you use with Tor
since your session may becompromised. Here is what you can do:
Option 1
Pay for a VPN anonymously
This means no credit cards. No
verified phone calls. No links to you or
anyone you know. In fact, leave no
money trail to your real name or city or
livelihood at all and never connect to the
VPN without Tor.For optimal anonymity, connect to
your VPN through Tor using Tails. Even
if the VPN logs every session, if you
always use Tor with Tails, it would
take an extremely well-funded adversary
to crack that security chain. Without
logging, it's even more secure.
But always assume they log.
Option 2
Pay for a VPN using a credit cardConnecting with Tor when using a
card with your name on it does nothing
for anonymity. It's fine for privacy, but
not for anonymity. This is good if you
want to use Pandora in Canada for
instance but not if you want to hire a
contract killer to loosen Uncle Frick's
lips a bit. Uncle Frick, who is 115 years
of age and being tight-lipped on where
the sunken treasure is.
Ahem, anyway, VPN services

sometimes get a bad rap by anonymityenthusiasts, but signing up anonymously
for a VPN has advantages. It strengthens
the anonymity when using Tor, for one.
Even if the VPN keeps logs of every
user, they will not know even with a
court order the real identity of the user in
question. Yet if you used Paypal,
Bitcoin, credit cards or any other
identifiable payment methods to
subscribe to a VPN for the express
purpose of using Tor, then anonymity is
weakened since these leave a paper trail
(Bitcoin by itself is not anonymous).But the real down and dirty gutter
downside is .onion sites. These are sites
that can only be accessed by using Tor.
The problem is that the last link of
connectivity for these sites needs to be
Tor, not the VPN. You'll understand what
is involved once you connect with one
which brings up our next question.
How Tor Friendly is the VPN?
That depends on you. Spammers useTor. Hackers use Tor. Identity thieves
use Tor. A few VPNs have reservations
about letting users attain 100%
anonymity by signing up anonymously.
But if you signed up anonymously then
you have little to fear since at that point
it is their ass on the line.
Only there is one problem: the
hardliners at the FBI do not like this
attitude. In fact, they'd just as soon go
after you if you use a VPN over Tor.
Might a person come under twice the
suspicion by using both? Maybe.

From Fee.org
"The investigative arm of the
Department of Justice is attempting to
short-circuit the legal checks of the
Fourth Amendment by requesting a
change in the Federal Rules of
Criminal Procedure. These procedural
rules dictate how law enforcement
agencies must conduct criminal

prosecutions, from investigation to
trial. Any deviations from the rules can
have serious consequences, includingdismissal of a case. The specific rule
the FBI is targeting outlines the terms
for obtaining a search warrant.
It's called Federal Rule 41(b), and
the requested change would allow law
enforcement to obtain a warrant to
search electronic data without
providing any specific details as long
as the target computer location has
been hidden through a technical tool
like Tor or a virtual private network. It
would also allow nonspecific search
warrants where computers have beenintentionally damaged (such as through
botnets, but also through common
malware and viruses) and are in five or
more separate federal judicial districts.
Furthermore, the provision would allow
investigators to seize electronically
stored information regardless of
whether that information is stored
inside or outside the court's
jurisdiction.
The change may sound like a
technical tweak, but it is a big leap
from current procedure."The NSA does this without
hindrance. We know this from
Snowden's leaks that the FBI uses the
NSA's metadata from private citizen's
phone records. Thus, a VPN is not a
truly formidable obstacle to them.
But this takes it to an entirely
different level since if merely signing up
for a VPN provides a basis for a legal
search, then they can snoop on any ISP's
server they want with no legal grounds
at all to justify it. They've done similarthings in Brazil.
But here in the good ole U.S. of A, it
usually goes down like this:
1.) Spy on JoBlo to see what he's up
to.
2.) Make justification to seize
PC/Raid/Data by reconstructing case
3.) Apply pressure to the right

people with direct access to subscriber
info4.) Subpoena to decrypt subscriber's
data. If they've done it once, they can do
it a hundred more times. No Big Deal.
Solution:
If you're going to go the VPN route,
then use PGP: Pretty Good Privacy.
Never, ever transmit plain data over a
VPN, not even one that offers SSL.
Final thoughts:1.) Talking to police will never help
you. Even in a raid situation. They
(Homeland, possibly) wake you at
gunpoint at 6AM and corral your family
and threaten to take everyone to jail
unless someone confesses. It's all lies,
all the time by these agencies. A friend
once remarked that a plain-clothes
officer once knocked on his door to ask
him if he was using Tor, only to make
sure he wasn't doing anything illegal.
He answered yes, but nothing illegal sir.
That gave incentive to go forward like agiant lawnmower right over his
reputation. He was proven innocent later
on but not before the cops dragged that
man's reputation through the mud. No
public apology came (Do they ever?).
2.) If they don't charge you for
running a hidden service, walk out. In
fact, if they don't charge you with
anything... walk out. Every word out of
your mouth will aid them, not you.
3.) You have no reason to justify
anything done in your own home to them,or anywhere else. The responsibility to
prove guilt is theirs, not yours.
But, if you are in a situation where
you have to talk or give up your
encrypted laptop, always always give up
your laptop first. Laptops are cheap and
easy to replace. Five years is not.Using Bitcoins to Signup Anonymously
to a VPN Service
Bitcoins are not designed for
absolute anonymity, but neither are
VPNs. They're designed for privacy, yes.
So why use them?
Well, because any extra layer that

strengthens your anonymity is a layer you
want. But just as with any advanced tool,
you can lessen anonymity if you arecareless with it. Good, tight anonymity
tools can be a bane or a boon: A boon
provided you do your homework. If not,
folly and embarrassment ensues,
possibly a situation where, depending on
the country you're in, you might as well
slap the cuffs on yourself. It's sad that the
times have come to this predicament.
So let's consider then how one pays
for a VPN and obtains this level of
absolute anonymity... recognizing that a
VPN by itself will do nothing to further
this goal. It is only one tool in a toolboxfull of tools and Bitcoin is only one of
them as well. You wouldn't try to repair
a Camaro engine with only a wrench,
would you?
Now then, about Bitcoin...
Bitcoins are open source coins, a
digital currency that utilizes P2P-like
code, and like real money you can buy
online products with it. Products like
memory cards at Newegg or even a
Usenet or VPN premium service. These
are useful to us. Using these Bitcoins,you the end-user, completely bypass the
need for a credit union or bank. Pretty
neat. But, they're not without their
shortcomings. More on that in a moment.
For now simply know that they are
created from the collective CPU
computations of a matrix of users (like
you, for instance) who donate to their
creation. Bitcoin mining is involved, and
though you may have seen images of
Bitcoins on websites stamped with a
golden "B", they are actually not
something you can carry around in yourpocket.
Not in the way you think, at least.
They have something in common
with PGP - public and private keys - just
like the PGP application, only instead of
verifying your identity like PGP does,
Bitcoins verify your balance. This is
where Bitcoin wallets come in. Again,

not a magic bullet but rather one tool at
our disposal.
On that point, Bitcoin Wallets willonly get better at strengthening
anonymity in the coming years. They
will accomplish this by breaking the
trail to our real identities. Oh, and their
development is constantly improving.
However as we mentioned earlier--
embarrassment will result if you neglect
to do your homework, for every
purchase by a particular wallet can be
traced. That's right. If you buy a new
video card at Newegg with it, the same
that holds your credit card details, and
then subscribe to a Usenet service orVPN, guess what... you've now
established a trail to your real identity.
The FBI or Chinese government will not
need baying bloodhounds to sniff you
out.
But not if you make only one
purchase per wallet.
This means never using it for *any*
online entity in which you've purchased
goods while your real IP is connected. It
also means forgoing Google Plus,
Facebook, Skype and all social mediaoutlets with said wallet. Twitter, Wal-
Mart, BestBuy and even small mom &
pop stores with multi-social media
buttons splattered all over their
websites--these are enemies of
anonymity whether they know it or not
(more likely they don't). They are not our
friends anymore than a grenade is your
friend after pulling the pin.
A single individual might hold
several addresses and make only two
purchases a year, but if he cross-
contaminates by mixing up (eachtransaction is recorded in the Bitcoin
blockchain), then anonymity is weakened
and in most cases, destroyed by his own
making. Not good.
The trick is this: don't create a
pattern. A string of purchases create a
pattern; the exact sort of pattern Google
and Amazon code into their algorithms

to search and better target you with
interest-based ads. Bad for anonymity
and that's far from the worse that can
happen. We get around this problem by using
Bitcoin mixers. These weaken the links
between several different Bitcoin
addresses since the history of that
purchase is wiped by the exchange of
Bitcoins among other Bitcoin users.
There are a few options available to
you. One is BitFog but there are many
others. Bitcoin Wallets
In order to subscribe to a VPN or
buy anything online with Bitcoins, a
Bitcoin wallet is required. More than
one type is available to us. We'll go
through each and list their pros and cons.

Desktop Wallet

This is what I use and for good
reason: I have absolute control over it
not to mention the thought of having to access my money on someone else's web
server defeats the entire idea of
anonymity. I would never store my
encrypted files "in the cloud" and neither
should you. At least, not without an
insanely secure system.
Think about it. Would you bury your
safe in the neighbor's yard with a For
Sale sign out front? Same deal. The
server could go down. The company
could go bankrupt. Any person on the
other end on the hosting side can install
a keylogger without your knowledge. Nasty buggers, those things. Desktop
wallets aren't perfect, mind you, but they
are better than The Cloud. One
downside is that you must backup your
Bitcoin wallet, an especially imperative
task if it contains a lot of money. I do
this quite religiously every week, as
should you. Apologies if this all sounds
like a Sunday sermon, but some of this
stuff really must be taken as gospel.

Mobility/Travel Wallet

As the name implies, you carry this on you to make purchases in the same
way you would a credit card.

Convenience x 1000.
There are many types of wallets such
as Coinbase and Electrum but I found
Multibit to be very easy to learn. It is
available in both Linux and Windows
and offers a pass phrase option. Even the
balance sheet looks like a PGP interface,
but yet is beginner-friendly and open-
source, so no backdoors. Good for
anonymity.Multibit Windows Install
Now we come to the instructions for
a clean install of this work of wonder.
Download the Windows installer
from this link.
Run the installer.
The possible problems we may run
into: On Windows 7 64-bit which is the
system of choice outside of Linux thesedays, it may be that the Java Virtual
Machine (JVM) is not correctly located,
or "Failed to create a selector" is shown
in the error message. A solution is to
change the compatibility setting:
Choose the compatibility dialog
(right click--> icon - Properties -->
Compatibility)
Choose: "Run this program in
compatibility mode for Windows XP
SP3."
Check the box: "Run this program
as an administrator"Multibit Linux Install
If you're a Linux fan (and you should
be if anonymity is something you strive
for), then download the Linux / Unix
installer.
Open a terminal window and create
an installer executable with:
chmod +x multibit-0.5.18-linux.jarRun the installer: java -jar multibit-
0.5.18-linux.jar
Install.
Thereafter you will have a shortcut
to start MultiBit in your "Applications |
Other" menu. If you see no MultiBit
shortcut, you can run MultiBit manually
by doing the following:
open a terminal window and 'cd'

to your installation directory
type java -jar multibit-exe.jarNow it is time to purchase Bitcoins.
There are a few useful guides around
which list possible advantages unique to
your geography.
As you can see from the link, there
are several options but what we want to
do is execute an offline option; to buy
Bitcoins off the grid which cannot be
traced. Cash n' carry.
LocalBitcoins looks promising asdoes TradeBitcoin. But as Trade looks
down so let's go with LocalBitcoins.
- After you choose a Bitcoin outfit,
you must signup for the site
(anonymously) but be aware of the
interest charges which vary from one to
another depending on how much you
want to deal in. For this transaction, use
an email in which you anonymously
signed up. That means:
- Tor Browser/Tails
- No Facebook or other SocialMedia/Search cookies present on
machine
- Only accessed for Tor/Bitcoins.
Choose 'Purchase' on the seller's
page and the amount we wish to buy.
Remember, we're not buying a house
here, only a VPN to use with Tor. Once
funds are transferred out of escrow, you
will be notified.
Notice that the trader you are dealing
with might be able to see your financial
information, i.e. which bank you use,etc., but you can always opt to meet up
in person if you want. This carries a
whole other set of risks.
Check to make sure the funds are in
your Bitcoin Wallet.Paying for the VPN to Use with Tor
Now it is time to pay for your VPN
service... anonymously. Let's choose Air
VPN at $9/mo and who also accepts
Bitcoins for payment.
First: Sign up for the service but do
not put any information that you've used
on any other site such as usernames or
passwords. Also, since we do not need

to input any banking info, no money trailwill be traced to us. The email we use is a throwaway email (you did use Tor to signup, right?)
Second: Give them the wallet address for our Bitcoin payment. Hit send.
Done!
Like any Usenet service, a VPN service will send confirmation to your email with details you need to use thatservice. Afterward you can see the details of this payment in your Bitcoin wallet.
As you can see, a Ph.D in Computer Science is not needed for this extra layer of anonymity. The problem with the mass of people on Tor, however, is that they cannot be bothered to do these simple extra steps. That's bad for them. Good for you. Those that wear extra armor are often the ones left standing after a long battle. But there is one topic left to discuss, and it's the most important:

Using Your Real Name Online Outside of Tor
This is a big one. One that I'm guilty of breaking because even anonymity nuts can crack under peer pressure every now and then and do something dumb like use Facebook over Tor (my early days, thankfully). A question I kept asking back then was this:
What kind of danger is there inusing your real name online?
Well sir, it depends.
Law enforcement and prospective employers who mine your social media presence for data are often worse than thieves who salivate when you announce on Twitter you'll be out of town for two weeks. Thieves, while unsavory and criminally deviant to be sure, rarely profess to be just. And thieves, as stated before, come in all shapes and sizes. If they take your private data withoutasking you first, that's stealing.
Employers can be the worst of the

lot, as hypocritical as Harvey Two-Face,
demanding transparency in your life but
not their own. Make an inflamed
political post or drink wine on vacation
in Bora Bora with half-naked Filipinas
twirling fire sticks and you could lose
your job... or be denied one. Not
kidding. Mention you use Tor and you
may hear your interviewer ask:
"I noticed you're a big fan of Tor.Could you elaborate on why you need
to use an anonymizing service? We like
transparency in our employees."
Yes, I was actually asked this in an
interview for a position that handled a
lot of money. It came out of nowhere, but
what really bothered me was the casual
way it was asked, like every applicant
should have something to hide if they
desire anonymous communications.
Maybe I was some rabid fan of Jason
Bourne and up to no good. At any rate,
they did not like my answer."Because I value freedom."
I came out of that interview
perplexed, yet jobless, viewing privacy
as somewhat of a double-edged sword
since one needs an online presence for
many higher paying employers. It did not
sit well with me. I felt a little cheated to
be honest and as I drove home, some of
the mumblings I overheard later on
became as loud as roaring trains in my
ears:Don't like someone on Facebook?
You probably won't like working with
them.
Like the competitor's products?
Here's our three-year non-compete
agreement for you to sign.
You use Tor? The only people that
use that are terrorists, pedos and hitmen.
Soon thereafter, any time a
prospective employer noticed "Tor"
under the Hobbies section of my resume,it would always illicit a negative
reaction. My breathing would become
erratic as my heart raced, as if they were
about to summon an unbadged

"authority" to warn me of being too
private.
He would dress a lot like Dilbert,
only he'd be skinnier, and with a
bumblebee-yellow pen and a clipboard.
He'd have multiple facial tics and a
quirky habit of raising a Vulcan eyebrow
as if it were purely illogical to value
privacy. I have no idea why he'd have a
clipboard, but he always did.My solution was to rightly divide my
public and private identity in social
settings and remove any trace of it on my
resume. In fact, I did not give any
indication on any social media site,
either, that I was into any of the
following:
- PGP
- Encryption, or encrypting files or
Operating Systems
- Tor Relays
- I2P- Freenet
- Anonymity in general
- Anything linking to Edward
Snowden
Such is the nature of the masses. One
simply cannot rely on Facebook or
Twitter or Google to respect one's
freedom to use Tor without announcing it
to the whole world.
But with Tor, Google cannot mine
your browsing session for ads. No ads =
no soup for them. From NBC:"The Internet search giant is
changing its terms of service starting
Nov. 11. Your reviews of restaurants,
shops and products, as well as songs
and other content bought on the Google
Play store could show up in ads that
are displayed to your friends,
connections and the broader public
when they search on Google. The
company calls that feature "shared
endorsements."
So I firewall everything I do. I useGhostery for social sites and offer only
pseudonymous details about myself. In
fact, I try to avoid any correlation

between Tor and any social media site
just as one would a can of gasoline and a
lighted match.Anonymous Bullies
The media along with Google and
Facebook seems to think that if only
everyone's name were known to them,
then every bully from California to
Florida would go up in smoke.
Vampirism, like bullying, comes in
many forms, but if you've ever read
Anne Rice then you know every clan is
as different as diamonds are to lumps ofcoal. But they do usually share similar
beginnings. Take adolescence for
example.
Were you ever bullied in school?
I was. I remember every buck
toothed spiked-club wielding ogre who
pelted me into nothing but a wet
snowball in 7th grade, and it didn't stop
there. How I wished it had, but not
having Aladdin's lamp made things
difficult. I watched as they spread like
cancer, sludging upward to other gradesfor easier victims. Ninth on upward to
12th and even into the workforce.
Bullies who'd make great orc chieftains
if there were any openings, such was
their cruelty and ire.
I recall one particularly nasty breed
of ogre in 8th grade. He was the worst of
the lot. A walking colossus who sweat
when he ate as though he were being
taken over by something in The Thing.
Either that or Mordor. He certainly had
the arms for it. When he arced an arm
over me it sounded like a double-bladedaxe slicing the air in half.
Harassment grew more fierce and
fiery every year. Later I would learn that
his entire family, perhaps his entire
generation, grew up being the baddest
of the bad - bullies that thrived on
terrorizing to make a name for
themselves. Every one of them went on
to become cops in the New Orleans
area. One died of diabetes. Another
went on to join the ATF to fight the evil

scourge called drugs (how'd that workout?).
I knew everything about these cretins
and not just their names. I knew who
their parents were. What they did for a
living. Who they hung out with. What
beers their dad's drank and with what
porn mags. Gossip spread like wildfire
in high school and no detail of
identifying information was ever left out.
And yes, I told the principle, a great
big lady named Beverly whose former
job was working in some HR high-rise. Iremember multiple times meeting her in
that office where glitzy awards hung like
a safari hunter's office and thinking if
only she had an elephant gun I could
borrow. Boom! My trouble's be over (so
thought the 13 year old).
Meetings between my circus acrobat
mother became fruitless and rather
embarrassing. Absolutely nothing
positive came of it. The point, however,
isn't that nothing came of it, but that
nothing came of it even as I knew
everything about the scourge I faceddaily. Knowing their identities did
NOTHING. Knowing their names did
nothing. Knowing how many other kids
they tormented did nothing and, let's face
it, kids just aren't smart enough to band
together and attack (despite how many
times we watched Road Warrior).
We can see how bullying spreads on
Facebook. Like anthrax. Little wolves
ostracize a rejected member when a
drop of fear is shown, so they crucify
without knowing much of anything about
him or why he's being targeted. Realnames? Check. Real addresses? Yep.
Everything is traceable now just as it
was way back then. And still the orcs
come in a blood-toothed frenzy like
sharks to a wounded dolphin.
When 13 year olds begin hanging
themselves in mom's bedroom to escape
the torture, one thing is immediately
obvious: what they really want is to
disappear. They want anonymity.

But that's not something bullies think
highly of. They won't allow it. Neitherdo they allow running away, not that a
kid has the means anyway: No money.
No car. No distant relatives in Alaska to
run and live with and hunt moose all
winter.
Anonymity, therefore, is not an
option. It's a requirement for sanity. It
should be the law on some level, but
isn't. This is because if they gave us true
anonymity, they would lose the precious
power they wield over us. If Google and
Facebook ever teamed up with the
federal government to require ID toaccess the internet, we'd all be better off
going face-to-face with an Alaskan
grizzly.Email Anonymity
There was a time when we didn't
have to worry about what we said in
emails. Security? That was something
geeks did. Geeks and supergeeks who
attended hacker conventions and scoured
Usenet for zero-day exploits. It was the
days of Altavista and Infoseek, when
Google was still wet behind the ears and
Microsoft was still struggling to satisfyevery Dos user's whim. We wrote
whatever we wanted and hit send with
nary a worry about third parties
intercepting it and using our own words
against us. Sadly, no longer.
Advertising and search engines now
tailor advertisements to individuals
based on what you like and are sure to
click. Trails are left. Messages are
scanned. And Gmail is no different than
Yahoo or Microsoft. In fact, judges
wield more power with the pen than any
CEO in any company in North America.When a trailer is leaked or someone
says something nasty about the
government, you can bet IP addresses
will be subpoenaed. Sometimes I
imagine a lot of ex-Soviet officers are
laughing at how many snitches the
Internet produces on a yearly basis.
Subversion to the extreme.
But... is it possible to send a

message that is foolproof against subpoenas?There are, in fact, many flavors to choose from to accomplish this task. Below are a few rock-solid services. Combined with Tor, they grant you a virtual fortress. Anonymity squared if your message is encrypted.
The first is TorGuard.TorGuard allows users to use PGP (Pretty Good Privacy) in email so you needn't worry about snooping. You get 10MB plus several layers of protection with mobility support.Second is W3, The Anonymous Remailer
Connectable with Tor, you only need an email address to send the message to (preferably encrypted with PGP--more on that in a moment).Another is Guerrilla Mail. They allow users to create throwaway emails to be used at leisure. Emails sent are immediately wiped from the system after you hit Send. Well, within one hour at any rate.All of these services claims ofanonymity would be pretty thin if we did not encrypt our messages-- which brings us to PGP.
PGP is the encryption standard of choice for many old users like myself, and for good reason. It has never been cracked by the NSA or FBI or any intelligence agency and likely won't until quantum computers become common. It works by way of key pairs, one which is public and one private (the one you will use to decrypt your messages with).Worry not about the term "keys". It is not difficult to grasp and will be as easy as hitting send once you've done it a few times.
The first thing you must do is make your public key available. This is onlyused to verify your identity and is not the same as divulging your passphrase for say, a Drivecrypt container. Your recipient must also share with you their key so you can respond in turn.
The good news?
Only the two of you will be able to read each other's messages. The caveat

is if the other person is compromised
and you don't know about it. They will
read everything you encrypt. Here is
what you need to know:1.) To begin, make two keys, one
public--for everyone else but you--and
one that you wouldn't even share with
your own mother. You should back this
key up in a secure medium, and
remember that if it isn't backed up to
three different types of media, it isn't
backed up. If your truly paranoid, send
one on an encrypted microSD to your
parents in case of housefire. Yes, it does
happen.
2.) If however you opt to tell mom,then she will need your public key (you
did publish it on a public key server,
right?) Then you can read it by way of
your private key. She doesn't know this
key (thank the gods!)
3.) You can "sign" any message you
want over Tor or anywhere else
(Freenet, for example, the highest
security setting of which demands
absolute trust of your friend's darknet
connection) to verify it is really you
sending it....Unless Norman Bates does a
shower scene on you and takes your
keys. Your mom can then verify with
your public key that it is really you.
4.) Users you've messaged with (or
not) can sign your public key as a way of
verifying your identity. As you can see,
the more people that do this, that is,
vouch for you, the better.
Important:Unless you've got the photographic
memory of Dustin Hoffman in Rainman,
it's a good idea to store your
public/private keys and passwords and
also revocation-certificate to backup
media so you can retrieve it five years
down the line... should you need it. And
believe me, you will!
Encrypt them in containers. Always
print your key-file or pass phrase and
deposit in a safe place. If you lose it, all

documents encrypted with it are
permanently lost. There are no back-doors and no way to decrypt without it.
Also, consider making an expiration date
at key-pair creation.
If you like nice and easy interfaces,
try Mymail-Crypt for Google's Gmail. It
is a plugin that allows users to use PGP-
encrypted messages in a handy interface,
though ensure your browser is air-tight
secure and you trust it with your private
key.
One other thingRather than having to encrypt files
and upload them somewhere unsafe,
look at AxCrypt encryption tool. This is
useful if you're used to uploading to
Dropbox or Google Drive. Just
remember that in the event you upload an
encrypted file to "The Cloud," you will
not know it if your password to said file
has been compromised without setting
strict security rules.
With that said, let's configure PGP
for Windows- Install Gpg4Win
- Next, create your key in Kleopatra
and choose Export-Certificate-to-Server
by right click so you can publish it to a
keyserver. Get a trusted friend to "sign"
and establish trust.
- Use Claws-Mail client that comes
packaged with it or use Enigmail if
you're using Thunderbird.
- Send a few messages back and
forth to your trusted friend via PGP toget the hang of things.
- Optionally you can set a
Yahoo/Gmail/Hotmail filter so as to
forward any messages that contain
"Begin PGP message" to a more private
account.

Tor Instant Messaging Bundle
It is no secret that the NSA has
Skype, Yahoo Chat and other instant
message services in their hands, but as
long as the Tor development team knows
about it, they can do something about it.

Enter Tor Instant Messaging Bundle.
True anonymity is the goal of this
application. It is built by the very samewho developed the Tor browser bundle
and like that application, will route all
communication through Tor relays...
encrypted backwards and forwards and
hidden from the NSA's prying eyes.
There is also Torchat.
Torchat, like Yahoo's IM, offers
encrypted chat and even file-sharing.
Since it is built upon Tor, you are
assured absolute privacy on what you
say and to whom you say it. Both
Windows and Mac versions areavailable and no install is necessary.
Just unzip anywhere and run (preferably
from an encrypted hard drive or USB-
Drive) the blue earth symbol titled
'Torchat'.
A few more useful apps:
ChatSecure - ChatSecure is mainly
used for encrypted messaging on
mobility devices but they offer PC,
Linux and Mac versions as well. From
their website:The Guardian Project creates easy
to use secure apps, open-source
software libraries, and customized
mobile devices that can be used around
the world by any person looking to
protect their communications and
personal data from unjust intrusion,
interception and monitoring.
Whether your are an average
citizen looking to affirm your rights or
an activist, journalist or humanitarian
organization looking to safeguard your
work in this age of perilous globalcommunication, we can help address
the threats you face.
Telegram - This app also focuses on
messaging but with superior speed and
is similar to SMS and allows for
picture/video sending. There are also
'Secret Chats' that offer encrypted
sessions. They claim no data is kept on
their servers and you can even set the
app to permanently delete all messages.

CryptoCat - Billed as an alternative
to social media chat apps like those seenon Facebook, Twitter and the like,
CryptoCat gives you encrypted
communications using the AES
encryption standard. All encrypted info
is deleted after an hour of inactivity.
Freenet - This is the granddaddy of
all anonymous systems the world over,
both for file sharing or any kind of secret
chats. Explaining everything it has to
offer goes far beyond our Tor discussion
as they are two different systems, but I
include it here as an alternative if youfind Tor lacking.
And it is not as simple as Tor, nor is
it as fast unless you leave it running
24/7. It is not for everyone as there are
all manner of criminal entities that use it
and you will notice this if you load up
any groups. It is hard to ignore and
unlike Usenet, there is no one to file a
complaint with. No one to report. It is
anarchy multiplied many times over in
many groups, but there are ways of
mitigating the damage.But for absolute anonymity and
freedom of speech, there is no better tool
to use if you have the patience to learn
its darknet offerings.
From the website:
Freenet is free software which lets
you anonymously share files, browse
and publish "freesites" (web sites
accessible only through Freenet) and
chat on forums, without fear of
censorship. Freenet is decentralised to
make it less vulnerable to attack, and ifused in "darknet" mode, where users
only connect to their friends, is very
difficult to detect.
Communications by Freenet nodes
are encrypted and are routed through
other nodes to make it extremely
difficult to determine who is requesting
the information and what its content is.
Users contribute to the network by
giving bandwidth and a portion of their
hard drive (called the "data store") for

storing files. Files are automaticallykept or deleted depending on how popular they are, with the least popular being discarded to make way for newer or more popular content. Files are encrypted, so generally the user cannot easily discover what is in his datastore, and hopefully can't be held accountable for it. Chat forums, websites, and search functionality, are all built on top of this distributed data store.

An important recent development, which very few other networks have, isthe "darknet": By only connecting to people they trust, users can greatly reduce their vulnerability, and yet still connect to a global network through their friends' friends' friends and so on. This enables people to use Freenet even in places where Freenet may be illegal, makes it very difficult for governments to block it, and does not rely on tunneling to the "free world".

It is not as simple as using a Usenet provider's newsgroup reader. No sir, Freenet requires patience. Using Frostor Fuqid (Front End apps for the main Freenet program), it might be half an hour before you can "subscribe" to groups or download in the way you can Usenet. Some groups, like the Freenet group and other technical groups will be immediately available, but with few messages. Time will solve this. So keep it running in the closet and forget about it for a day or so if you plan on subscribing to a lot of groups.

It will be worth the wait.Frost & Fuqid The two free front ends I recommend are: Frost and Fuqid.

Frost has seen a lot of improvements but I recommend you try Fuqid first as it is the first external app for Freenet that acts as as an insert/download manager for files. Fuqid stands for: Freenet Utility for Queued Inserts and Downloads and runs on Windows or

Linux under wine.The Fuqid freesite is on Freenet itself at:
USK@LESBxzEDERhGWQHl1t1av7 KHB-
W8HHi9dM,AQACAAE/Fuqid/-1/
You will need to paste the above into Freenet's front control panel where it says "Key". It can take several minutes to load if you're new to the system.
After you've installed it, right click on the left side with your list of boards and choose "Add new board". For the name put in "fuqid-announce" with out the quotes. You will now find a new board called "fuqid-announce" in your list of boards.
Right click this board and choose "Configure selected board". This will bring up a new window. On that window click "Secure board" to change it from a public board. Now in the section that says "Public key" paste in the key below:SSK@qoY-
E5SKRu66pmKH64xa~R~w3hXmS5ZNtq QE,AQACAAE
Now you have the announce board for Fuqid added to your Frost boards. The latest releases of Fuqid will be posted to this board along with the fuqid board on FMS. Questions? Direct them to the Frost or FMS board called Fuqid.Passwords
Good, strong passwords are like having a couple of Rottweilers sleeping in your den. Most intruders will leave when the chaos starts. Weak passwords are like having a Golden Retriever. Nice and friendly and easy to trust around kids, but might just let out a little woof at 3AM when said intruder comes. Then he will hide under the coffee table (the dog, not the intruder).I've heard for years that you should never use anything personal as your password. That includes family names. Favorite books. Movies. So what's the solution?
Remix your passwords with a

symbol or two. If you think a hacker
won't be able to guess the name of your
girlfriend's locker combination, you'd be
mistaken. It is dirt simple to guess even
if you mix it up a bit. Computers devoted
to this practice can guess many in lessthan a nanosecond.
But how do you remember a
password for a site used over Tor that
has symbols?
- Easy. Use a passphrase that is
simple to recall for you only. First write
out the first letter of each word, taking
not of case and position. Insert symbols
therein. For instance:
Last Sunday, the wife bought me a
Rolex watch and it was too ugly.Which when changed is:
LS,twbmarwaiw2u
The above pass is hard for a hacker
to guess but easy for you to remember...
assuming you are good at substitution.

Changing Your Passwords

Provided you've followed the aboveto the letter, you shouldn't have to rotate
out your passwords every 90 days. I'm
sure you've heard from both sides of the
aisle their say on the subject, but I
believe research has proven that keeping
a strong password (unless proof of
compromise) is a safe bet.
The research paper from ACM/CCS
2010: "The Security of Modern
Password Expiration: An Algorithmic
Framework and Empirical Analysis" by
Yinqian Zhang, Fabian Monrose and
Michael Reiter came to the conclusionthat changing passwords every few
months did not, repeat, did NOT
increase security:
at least 41% of passwords can be
broken offline from previous passwords
for the same accounts in a matter of
seconds, and five online password
guesses in expectation suffices to break
17% of accounts.
....our evidence suggests it may be
appropriate to do away with password
expiration altogether, perhaps as aconcession while requiring users to

invest the effort to select a significantly
stronger password than they would
otherwise (e.g., a much longer
passphrase). ....
In the longer term, we believe our
study supports the conclusion that
simple password-based authentication
should be abandoned outright.
Storing Passwords in Tor BrowserYou may have noticed that the
"Remember Password" option in Tor
Browser is not available, or so it seems.
But if you look at the privacy setting and
alter the history setting to "remember
history" and "remember passwords for
sites," it will no longer be greyed out.
Diceware
If you must store passwords, a good
option for a unique random one is
Diceware, (there are others, too) whereyou can get an expire date for any
password months from the date of
creation. You can copy any password to
a text file then encrypt it and mail it to
yourself or place on a removable
(encrypted) drive or USB stick.
Remember: Tor does nothing to
improve the security of your *system* to
everyday attacks. It only improves
security online, and even then only when
used responsibly. Tor has no idea if your
version of Windows is unpatched andinfected with a zero-day malware
payload that infected it with a keylogger.
One way in which a hacker could
guess your complex password is if they
linked your Tor usage with non-Tor
usage and compromised your passwords
from a non-Tor site. This is why you
should never use the same
usernames/passwords for Tor that you
do for non-Tor activity.
Preventing Non-Tor Activity FromBeing Linked with Tor Activity
It is risky to browse different
websites simultaneously and preserve
anonymity since Tor might end up
sending requests for each site over the
same circuit, and the exit node may see

the correlation.

It is better to browse one site at a time and thereafter, choose "New Identity" from the Tor button. Any previous circuits are not used for thenew session.

Further, if you want to isolate two different apps (allow actions executed by one app to be isolated from actions of another), you can allow them to use the same SOCKS port but change the user/pass.

Another option is to set an "isolation flag" for the SOCKS port. The Tor manual has suggestions for this but it will lead to lower performance over Tor. Personally I like to use Whonix.Two instances, two VMs. One of them runs Tor and the other with Tor Firefox.Keyloggers

You might wonder what a keylogger has to do with Tor. Or for that matter, what a keylogger even is. You're not alone. In fact you'd be surprised how many people don't know and shocked how many techs consider them a non-issue.

In 2010 I caught up with an old childhood friend of mine I had not seenin over a decade. He was now an ATF agent. I was surprised and (falsely) assumed his extensive training meant he knew as much as an NSA agent when it came to computer security. Wrongo.

He replied to a post I made on a Facebook regarding the hacking group "Anonymous."

"What's a keylogger?" he asked. I waited for someone else to reply. No one did so I told him. He seemed amazed, dumbfounded, as though it weresomething only recently unleashed upon the net. I then told him that they had been around a long time.

But (sigh), there's a lot of confusion on what they do exactly. Some people call them spyware. Others say they're trojans. Still others, exploits. They're a little bit of everything to be honest. They are surveillance software that

tracks and records every click you make,
every website visited, every keystroke
typed. Chats, Skype, Emails. If you cantype it, it can record it and all right
under your very nose. It can even email
what you type to a recipient on the other
side of the world. CC numbers,
passwords and Paypal login details are
just the short list of targets it can
acquire.
So how does one get in infected?
- Opening an email attachment
- Running an .exe file from a P2P
network from an untrusted user
- Accessing an infected website withan outdated browser
- The NSA, if they can grease the
right palms
Some employers use them to track
productivity of employees. Some wives
attach one via USB (Hardware version)
to see who their hubbies are conversing
with at night after bed. Parents use them
on the kid's computer. So it isn't like
they're 100% malicious all the time.
But they are devilishly difficult to
detect. They wield an almost vampiricpresence, but like vampires there are
subtle signs you can glean without
whipping out a wooden stake.
Vampire Signs
- Sluggish browsing speed
- Laggy mouse/pausing keystrokes in
a text doc
- Letters don't match on display with
what you type
- Errors on multiple webpages when
loading heavy text/graphicsThere are two types:
Software Keyloggers
This type hides inside your operating
system. They lurrrve Windows. Linux,
not so much. The keylogger records
keystrokes and sends them to a hacker or
other mischief maker at set times
provided the computer is online.
Cloaked, most users will never see it
working its dark art. Many popular anti-
virus vendors have trouble identifying it

because the definitions change sofrequently.

Hardware Keyloggers

Bond might have used one of these.
\ Being hardware, it is a physical
extension that can plug into any USB on
a PC and can be bought online by
suspecting spouses or kids wanting
access to their dad's porn stash.
Keystrokes are logged to ram memory.
No install needed.Thus, unless you're the type to check
your PC innards every day, you might not
spot it until it's too late. They also can
be built right into the keyboard. The FBI
loves swapping the target's out with a
carbon copy custom-built surveillance
device. Granted, this is mainly for high-
value targets like the Mafia but they're
available to anyone.

For The Children...

Those that sell these usually do sounder the guise of protecting the
children. You know, keeping an eye on
them at all times like mom should be
doing. Problem is, what is good for the
goose is good for the gander and that
usually involves Big Brother lending a
helping hand. And not only him, either.
Thieves and hackers love these. That
means you must be all the more vigilant.
If a keylogger is installed, all encryption
is defeated. PGP, Tor, Freenet.
Everything is compromised and you must
do a full wipe of your hard drive andstart over, paying close attention to
whether you burned any media with
infected files - lest you be infected all
over again after a fresh OS install. If you
used the same password for BIOS entry
as anything else-- forum, websites,
Paypal-- you must change it immediately.

Keylogger Prevention

- Check your keyboard for
suspicious attachments. If you are an
employee at X company and a newkeyboard arrives at your desk one
morning, exercise caution unless you
trust your boss 200%.
- Use a Virtual Keyboard. No

keystrokes = no logging!
- Use Guarded ID to prevent hackers
from capturing your keystrokes. It works
by scrambling everything you type,
rendering any info useless to hackers.
- Use a decent firewall to stop a
keylogger from delivering your data. A year ago, my Comodo firewall alerted
me to suspicious network activity
seemingly out of nowhere when I wasn't
doing anything online. Turns out I had the
Win64/Alureon trojan. I had to use
Malwarebytes to detect and remove it.
Norton was useless! Imagine that.
Other Anti-Keyloggers
If you do not mind spending some
coin, there are a few more:Zemana AntiLogger (Free)
This "free" version is a bare-boneskeylogger-detector. In fact, it's quite
stripped down but if all you require is
being alerted then this might be for you.
The Keylog Guard offers encryption for
all things typed at the keyboard. Any
snooper will only get garbled letters
from you. The paid version is somewhat
pricey at $29.99 and comes with extra-
protection for malware and such but is a
bit overkill.
Also, it will nag you if you try and
run something safe it doesn't like, much
like every other anti-virus will.SpyShelter STOP-LOGGERThe Free version offers more than
Zemana does in that you get screenshot
capture. It will also alert you to any
code that tries to swipe your keystrokes
from you but the Free version is not 64-
bit compatible. It is $24.99.
Be aware, however, that removing a
keylogger is nasty business as they have
a habit of reinstalling themselves.
Keyloggers will often hide as a service
in svchost.exe so task manager isn't
much help without a dedicated app. Theoptimal way of prevention is to stop
them in their tracks before insertion.
Be proactive. Anticipate a password
compromise. Remember, vigilance!Darknet Markets
Some of you might be wondering

how safe a Darknet really is in light of
the vulnerabilities discussed. The short
answer is this: As safe as you make it.
You are the weak link. The last link
in the security chain. And although you
need Tor to access Onion sites, the term
can apply to any anonymous network -
networks like I2P or Freenet or anything
else that cloaks the source of datatransmit, and by extension, your identity.
Which brings us to the Darknet
Marketplace.
The complete list of such
marketplaces on the deep web are
numerous, and the risk of getting
scammed is quite high. It's one reason
why you may not have heard about them.
They are often taken down quickly by
either a venomous reputation or a law
enforcement bust. Sometimes they piss
off the wrong people and then spammersddos the site. But there are numerous
places one can go if you're curious about
what is sold by whom.
When I say sold, what I mean is...
Anything you want that cannot be gained
through the usual legal channels. And
remember that what is legal in one
country may be illegal in another. In
Canada, lolicon comics are illegal and
can get you in big trouble if you cross
the border. But not in America. In the
USA you can pretty much write any story
you want. In Canada? TEXT storiesinvolving minors are verboten.
The other difference is that there are
safety nets in buying almost anything in a
first world country on the open market.
Think BestBuy. Mom and Pop stores.
Florist shops. If customers get injured,
what happens? Customers sue via the
legal safety net and make a lot of
lawyers a lot of money.
But the Darknet Marketplace laughs
at any such safety nets. In fact, you're
likely to get scammed at least a few
times before finding a reputable dealerfor whatever goods you seek. And it
really doesn't matter what it is, either -

Teleportation devices? Pets? Exotic
trees? It's all the same that goes around.
Whatever is in demand will attract
unsavory types and not just on the
buyer's end.
Therefore, research any darknet
market with Tor, being careful to visit
forums and check updated information to
see if any sites have been flagged as
suspicious or compromised. Some other
advice:- Always use PGP to communicate.
- Never store crypto-currency at any
such marketplace.
- Assume a den of thieves unless
proven otherwise by *them*. The
responsibility is theirs just as it is
offline, to prove they are an honest
business. If you open your own, keep
this in mind: customers owe you nothing.
You can only betray them once.
Now for some examples of Phishers
and Scammers and other Con men. Bytheir fruits, ye shall know them.
1.) Silk Road 2.0
(e5wvymnx6bx5euvy...) Lots of scams
with this one. Much like Facebook and
Google emails, you can tell a fake
sometimes by the address. Paste the first
few letters into a shortcut next to the
name. If it doesn't match, steer clear.
2.) Green Notes Counter
(67yjqewxrd2ewbtp...)
They promised counterfeit money totheir customers but refuse escrow. A
dead giveaway.
3.) iPhones for half off:
(iphoneavzhwkqmap...)
Now here is a prime example of a
scam. Any website which sells
electronic gadgets on the deep web is
ripe for scamming customers. Whereas
in the Far East you will merely get
counterfeit phones with cheap, Chinese
made parts that break within a month, on
the Deep Web they will simply take yourmoney and say adios. Actually, they
won't even bother saying that.
So then, how does one tell a scam?

Because many new darknet vendors
will arise out of thin air, with rare
products that will make customers
swoon and send them money... without
doing any research on their name or
previous sales. A real hit and run
operation. Hit quick and fast and dirty.
Seduce as many as they can before the
herd catches on to the wolf in disguise.Many are suckered, thinking "it's only a
little money" but a little money from a
lot of Tor users goes a long way in
encouraging other scammers to set up
shop.
When you ask them why they do not
offer escrow, they say "We think it is
unreliable/suspicious/unstable" amid
other BS excuses. It is better to hold on
to your small change than leave a trail to
your treasure chest. And make no
mistake some of these scammers are like
bloodhounds where identity theft isconcerned.
- Do your research! Check forums
and especially the dates of reviews they
have. Do you notice patterns? Are good
reviews scattered over a long period of
time or is it rather all of a sudden--the
way some Amazon affiliate marketers do
with paid reviews that glow? Not many
reviews from said customers?
If you've seen the movie "Heat," with
Al Pacino and Robert de Niro, you know
when it is time to Walk Away. In themiddle of a nighttime heist, Niro goes
outside for a smoke. He hears a distant
cough. Now, this is middle of the night in
an unpopulated part of the city that
comes from across the street - a parking
lot full of what he thought was empty
trailers. Hmm, he thinks. Not so empty
(it was a cop). He walks back into the
bank and aborts.
The other aspect is time. Some fake
sites will set a short ship time and count
on you not bothering to see the sale as
finalized before you can whistle Dixieout of your ass. After finalization, you're
screwed since the money is in their

wallet before you can even mount a protest.Fraud Prevention

One is Google, believe it or not, at http://www.google.com/imghp. Dating sites like Cherry Blossoms and Cupid sometimes use reverse image search to catch fakers and Nigerian scammers masquerading as poor lonely singles to deprive men of their coinage. If they can catch them, so can you. If the image belongs to some other legit site, chances are it is fake. Foto Forensics also doesthe same, and reports metadata so that it becomes even harder to get away with Photoshop trickery.When it is Okay to FE (Finalize Early)

FE means 'Finalize Early'. It's use online can usually be found in black marketplaces like Silk Road and Sheep's Marketplace. It simply means that money in escrow is released before you receive your product. Every customer I've ever spoken with advises against this unless you've had great experience with that business.Buuut... Quite a few vendors are now making it a standard practice to pay funds up front before you have anything in your hands.

On more than one Marketplace forum, there's been heated exchange as to when this is proper. You might hear, "Is this guy legit? What about this Chinese outfit over here? He seems shady," and others: "A friend said this guy is okay but then I got ripped off!".

You get the idea.

Here is my experience on the matter.1.) It is okay when you are content with not getting what you paid for. This may seem counterproductive, but think how many gamblers go into a Las Vegas casino and never ask themselves "How much can I afford to lose?"

The answer, sadly, is not many. Vegas was not built on the backs of losers. Some merchants do not like escrow at all. Some do. So don't spend more than you can afford to lose. Look at

it the way a gambler looks at makingmoney.
2.) It is okay when you are
guaranteed shipment. There are FE
scammers out there that will give you an
angelic smile and lie right into your eyes
as they swindle you. Do not depend
solely on reviews. A guy on SR can be
the best merchant this side of Tatooine
and yet you will wake up one day and
find yourself robbed. He's split with a
million in BTC and you're left not even
holding a bag. Most won't do this to you.
But a few will.When it is NOT Okay to FE
- When losing your funds will result
in you being evicted or a relationship
severed. Never borrow money from
friends and especially not family unless
you want said family to come after you
with a double-bladed ax. If you get
ripped off, you lose not only the cash but
the respect and trustworthiness of your
family. Word spreads. You don't pay
your debts. What's that saying in Gameof Thrones?
Right. A Lannister always pays his
debts. So should you.MultiSigna
Sounds like something from
Battlestar Galactica to pass from ship to
ship. A badge of honor perhaps some
hotshot flyboy wears on his fighter
jacket that bypassed a lot of red tape.
While not exactly mandatory, it
makes for interesting reading, and is
something Tor users might want to know
about if they wish to make purchasesanonymously. Here's what happens:
When a purchase is enacted, the
seller deposits money (in this case,
Bitcoins) in a multi-signature address.
After this, the customer gets notification
to make the transaction ($,€) to the
seller's account.
Then after the seller relays to
MultiSigna that the transaction was a
success, MultiSigna creates a transaction
from the multi-signature address that
requires both buyer and seller so that itmay be sent to the network. The buyer

gets the Bitcoins and ends the sale.
Confused yet? I was too at first. You'll
get used to it.
Critical:
MultiSigna only exists as a
verifier/cosigner of the entire
transaction. If there is disagreement
between seller and buyer, no exchange
occurs. Remember the scene in
Wargames when two nuclear silo
operators have to turn their keyssimultaneously in order to launch? Yeah,
that.
MultiSigna will of course favor one
or the other, but not both if they cannot
mutually agree. The upside is that is if
the market or purchaser or vendor loses
a key, two out of three is still available.
A single key cannot spend the money in
2/3 MultiSig address.Is it safe? Is it secret?
I don't recommend enacting a million
dollar exchange for a yacht, or even a
thousand dollar one as they both carry
risk, but ultimately it is up to you. Just
remember that trust is always an issue on
darknets, and you're generally safer
making several transfers with a
seller/buyer who has a good history of
payment. In other words, reputation as
always, is everything.Alas, there are a few trustworthy
markets that have good histories of doing
things properly, thank heavens.
Blackbank is one. Agora is another.
Take a look at the Multi-Sig Escrow
Onion page here with Tor:
http://u5z75duioy7kpwun.onion/wiki/i
Sig_Escrow
SecurityNow then. You might be wondering
what the effect would be if a hacker
gained entry to the server. What mischief
might he make? What chaos could he
brew if he can mimic running a
withdrawal in the same manner that the
server does?

Well it's like this: If a hacker were to

gain access and attempt to withdraw money, a single-signature would be applied and passed to the second sig signer for co-signature. Then the securityprotocol would kick in where these policies would be enforced:

1.) Rate limits: the rate of stolen funds slows

2.) Callbacks to the spender's server: Signing service verifies with the original spender that they initiated and intended to make the spend. The callback could go to a separated machine, which could only contain access to isolated approved withdrawal information.3.) IP limiting: The signing service only signs transactions coming from a certain list of IPs, preventing the case where the hacker or insider stole the private key.

4.) Destination Whitelists: Certain very high security wallets can be set such that the signing service would only accept if the destination were previously known. The hacker would have to compromise both the original sending server as well as the signing service.Let me repeat that MultiSigna are never in possession of your bitcoins. They use 2 of 3 signatures (seller, buyer & MultiSigma) to sign a transaction. Normal transactions are signed by the seller and then by the buyer.

Purchaser Steps for MultiSig Escrow

1.) Deposit your Bitcoins. Purchase ability is granted after 6confirmations

2.) Make a private & public key (Brainwallet.org is a JavaScript Client-Side Bitcoin Address Generator)

3.) Buy item, input public-key & a refund BTC address (Luck favors!)

4.) Retrieve purchased item

5.) Input the private key and close

Below is a list of exchanges that support Multisig:

Bitstamp - Multisig service:

https://www.bitgo.comRock Trading - Multisig service:
https://greenaddress.it
TeraExchange - Multisig service:
https://www.bitgo.com
BitQuick - Multisig service:
https://www.bitgo.com
There is also this monster list:
http://bitcoinx.io/exchangesThe Long Arm of the Law
Can the law steal funds?
- Assuming you mean U.S. law, no...
since the wallet does not contain the
money. The Bitcoin blockchain prevents
this. Hackers cannot steal it either since
two private-keys are required and they
will have had to steal 2 out of 3 private
key holders... not likely.
What about safety in using theprivate key?
- Never irresponsibly use the private
key from your Bitcoin wallet. Create a
new one instead. Give it the same love
you give your Truecrypt/DiskDecryptor
master keys. Lots and lots of special
love that no one else gets.
This sounds awfully risky. Won't I
get caught?
Here is how most people get caught,
and it really matters not what it is. Youcould be dealing in illegal Furbies
(Believe it or not, back in 1999 the NSA
felt these toys might be able to record
highly-classified intel). Most dealers get
busted making the usual mistakes:
- Bar Bragging
- Dropping too much personal data
to strangers (See Ross Ulbricht)
- Selling contraband to undercover
law enforcement
- Snitches
- Committing crimes while under
surveillance- Managing an operation that grows
by leaps and bounds (with loads of
newbies making mistakes).
How far will the police go to catch
you? That's a good question. The answer
thought is pretty simple: As far as
resources allow. If they want you badly

enough but lack the funding, they'll rampup the threat you present to the media
and churches and synagogues and cold
call everyone begging for money to catch
you, you damned dirty ape!
Just kidding. It'll probably be no
worse than what Charleton Heston
suffered being hogtied and dragged
around the ape city. Some apes are
worse than others...usually the military
apes.
But really, it all boils down to if
whatever you're doing and if it is illegal,Furbies included. They really could care
less what it is as long as it grants the
department flashy headlines. Flashy
headlines mean more funding. More
funding = higher salaries. Bigger guns. If
not guns, then armor.
Case in point: In 2010, police in
L.A. organized a phony sweepstakes
scheme in order to lure in those with
outstanding warrants. I kid you not, they
did not come up with this idea
themselves, but rather took it from The
Simpsons.They sent out close to a thousand
fake letters under the name of a
marketing group only to have a little
over half a dozen show up at the La
Mirada Inn for their free prize: A BMW
238. Nice, eh? Only the joke was on
them as their smiles melted upon hearing
those four dirty words, "You're all under
arrest!"
The poor saps even brought ID to
verify their identities. Dumb. They might
as well have slapped on the cuffsthemselves. And if they're willing to go
through all that trouble just for a few
misdemeanor crimes, imagine what they,
along with the NSA, will do with a
group of Tor users selling Furbies!
And this is an OFFLINE example.
Imagine what one department can do by
lying alone to an ISP or search engine.
Threats of fines. Warrants. Bad
publicity. Subpoenas of users. A bad
reputation they are not likely to recover

from soon. Police in Vegas in particular
love to play dirty like this, dredging upold laws to ensure every member in that
Ferbie operation has the book thrown at
him.
In 2013, a Secret Service Agent
arrested several online by selling them
fake IDs. The kicker?
They were all charged under the
RICO Act of 1970. Originally created to
put away mobsters, it allows them to
lasso entire groups and charge each
individual as if he committed the same
crime everyone else in the group did...no matter the role.
Translation: The courier gets the
same treatment as the ringleader, as do
the buyers. Individually, not much prison
time in the grand scheme of things in
1970, but being charged as a GROUP?
Twenty years minimum. Al Capone
never saw such a hefty sentence.
It simply doesn't matter to a
prosecutor if you're OS is encrypted and
they can't get the data. All they need to
prove is that you were part of theenterprise operation. That can be done
outside of your shiny new Western
Digital hard drive by subpoena to your
ISP and a few other services you
subscribe to. They've done this (and
succeeded) with the newsgroup porn
bust years ago in which every member of
that hideous pedo group had encryption
coming out of their ears.
Here, according to "Grugq" at
Github, was the short list of rules in that
group.- Never reveal true identity to
another member of the group
- Never communicate with a member
of the group outside usenet
- Group membership remains strictly
within the confines of the Internet
- No member can positively identify
another
- Members do not reveal personally
identifying information
- Primary communications

newsgroup is migrated regularly
- If a member breaks a security
rule/fails to encrypt a message=BAN- Periodically reduce chance of law
enforcement discovery on each
newsgroup migration by:
- Creating new PGP key pair,
unlinking from previous messages
- Each member creates a new
nickname
- Nickname theme selected by
Yardbird (Group leader)
The affidavits read like a Hell's
Angels list of rules. And though I
disagree with his (the website owner,
not Yardbird) conclusion that "there arebasically no nice people who provide
case studies of OPSEC practices," I
believe much can be learned by studying
the habits of law-abiding citizen and
criminal alike, especially considering
the wide net over which the NSA is
casting over law abiding citizens.
Remember that in Nazi Germany, if
you slandered the SS, that was a capital
offense. The film 'Sophie Scholl' is an
excellent example of underground
resistance movement for the right reason.
It won accolades for its realisticportrayal of a college woman who stood
up to the SS elite and was beheaded for
it.
North Korea, 2015... same. They'd
have little issues with doing worse.
Beheading might be almost too lenient
for them as they prefer prolonged,
tortuous environments for their subjects.
China? China has done some strange
things, like outlawing stripping at
funerals and banning Bitcoin
transactions, and I do recall the violent
protests by Muslims in 2010 andthinking "Those communist schmucks
will round up all those screaming fools
and shoot them at dawn and not look
back!"
My Chinese girlfriend leaned over to
me as we watched and mumbled, "They
won't wait till dawn."I like to think of Darkcoin as

Bitcoin's smarter brother. Much smarter in fact, and darker. The best part of course being that it is constantly evolving.Like Bitcoin they are a privacy-centric digital money based on the Bitcoin design. It's a design that allows for anonymity as you make day-to-day purchases on, well, just about anything so long as the digital store offers it. With Bitcoin, anyone can see who made a purchase by only looking at the public blockchain. What Darkcoin does is anonymize your transaction further by using Master nodes - a decentralized network of servers that negate any requirement for third-parties: Partiesthat could scam you out of your coins. Though few outlets use it, it is one of the quickest growing digital currencies out there, with an economy breaching over twenty million. Impressive. And that's not all. It's "Darksend" feature is quite fascinating--increasing privacy by compounding a typical transaction with two other users.

Needless to say, this is immensely attractive to a lot of Tor users who value high anonymity. Whistleblowers,journalists, underground political movements. That's the good list. The bad list though, well, you can never have the good without the bad: Terrorists. Contract killers. Tax evaders. Fallout players with the child-killing perk. I hear the same arguments against its use that I heard with Freenet: Bad guys want to evade detection. Bad guys trade Darkcoins. You use Darkcoins. Therefore, you're a bad guy. Cue torches and pitchforks and black cats catapulted over the moat.Heroin dealers love to use cash yet you never hear news outlets screaming about cash-only users linking to such a crime. Besides, the most corrupt money launderers are the central banks. It is they that allow states to borrow from future citizens to pay today's debts. One

need only look at the National Debt to
realize this.
But that's not to say Darkcoins are
without issues. A few excellent
questions have arisen:
- What if these "Masternodes"
eventually form centralization?
- What if Darkcoin is abandoned by
the creators once the price goes through
the roof?
- Who is trustworthy enough to
"audit" Darkcoin? We saw an audit with
Truecrypt in 2013 which turned out to
show no backdoors... except that the
developers shut it down with a cryptic
message saying Truecrypt was NotSecure Anymore. We can argue all day
about what that meant.
These questions may never be
answered. But that should not stop us
from forging a new frontier in anonymity
services.Using Darkcoin for Business
It is much harder to run a Hidden Tor
Service than it is to open a business
using Darkcoin. It's so simple really that
it boggles the mind what might be
available in the future... and with
minimal risk to you.
If this appeals to you, then get the
Darkcoin Wallet. This is used to
send/receive/store Darkcoin with the
benefit of using Darksend for 100%anonymity. More info here on this. Most
of your patrons will want you to have a
wallet, so better to learn it early in the
business rather than later.
Pick a Transaction Processor
Below are a few you can research to
your liking. Not every processor will
suit everyone just as every bank or
credit union will not appeal to everyone.
You must judge these yourself, weighing
your needs with whatever risk yourbusiness entails. I've tried most of these
and came away satisfied but like
everything else with crypto currency,
what works for me may not work for
you.

AltAccept
FeesTransaction: 0.25% + 0.0005 DRK;
Withdrawal: 0.01 DRK
CoinPayments
Transaction: 0.50%; Withdrawal:
Network transaction fee (TX)CointoPay
Transactions: 0% (coin to coin)
0.5% (coin to fiat); Withdrawal:
Network transaction fee (TX)Transaction: 0.5%; Withdrawal:
Included with transaction fee
Some promo-graphics for your site,
or whatever else you're using to
advertise to your customers--you want
them to know you accept Darkcoins,
right?Darkcoin Graphics (courtesy of the
Darkcoin homepage)
After this you should signup to the
Merchant Directory.
Then (optionally), do some reading
on InstantX here. InstantX is a double
spend proof instant transaction method
via the masternode network. Not exactly
light reading, but the more you know...
Further thoughtsNo single entity has control of the
entire system. Though the chance of an
accident borders on the not bloody
likely, you need to remember that
Darkcoin is still in development and
because of that, unforeseen things
happen. So a healthy dose of due
diligence is required. I suggest only
purchasing with money that doesn't break
the bank in case bad luck happens upon
you.
Frequent backups are mandatory for
your wallet, more than Bitcoin since theanonymizing process executes more
transactions in the background. If you've
ever used Freenet, you know how slow
the network can be and how much of a
system resource hog anonymity often
requires. Thus, make a new backup of
your wallet whenever a you hit a coin
ceiling.Darknet OPSEC
"Three can keep a secret if two of
them are dead..."

- Ben Franklin

The above quote was a favorite of
mine in elementary school. It was
applicable then just as it is now to
having a secure mindset, and boy how I
loved spouting that line whenever a
friend begged me to confirm a rumorhe'd heard. A rumor that, if validated,
could have landed me in hot water with
my red-headed chem teacher. Luckily I
knew when to keep my mouth shut.
As you should.
Keeping your mouth shut about
Darknet markets is more important than
any encryption scheme you use,
passphrase you know, Freenet group key
or anything related to your Bitcoin
wallet. Knowledge is power.No, strike that. Knowledge is
potential power. And power in slippery
hands can be disastrous. Playing the bar
braggart might be fun after a few beers
and win you a few points with other
guys, but it gets more people imprisoned
over frivolous reasons than anything else
I can think of. And I've seen more than
one friend go down in flames because
they mentioned a darknet market to
someone they thought they could trust.
But then that friend told someone else he
trusted, more than anyone in the world.
We"ll call my friend Grady.Grady told his girlfriend. Spared no
details of his darknet ops and how they
traversed several continents. He made
himself sound like Agent Smith from the
Matrix. I shook my head upon hearing
this...
Cue Fred Sanford: "You Big
Dummy!"
Trusting her to keep his secret was
not just dumb, it was galactically stupid.
Like expecting Eve to eat the forbidden
fruit all by herself. And we know howthat story ends. Misery truly loves
company.
Next thing he knew, he attracted the
attention of the authorities in Hong Kong,
one of which was her father. The secret

was safe enough he supposed, until he refused to marry his hyper-critical girlfriend, claiming he had taken the "Red Pill" and feared settling down with an ultra-hardline feminist harpy (his words) would kill his dreams. Well it killed something alright. His freedom.Lesson? You can't fix stupid, so why would you trust it?

While you needn't go totally dark about your darknet knowledge for all eternity, in real life conversations, Social Media outlets, Tinder, Skype, etc., mums the word. Invoke radio silence where applicable or better yet, feign ignorance. If they show you proof, simply say you have good connections. Then buy them a beer and leave. If they still persist, consider warning them you're about to sever all connections tothem. Friends come and go, but freedom is priceless.How to Setup a Hidden Service on Tor

A benefit to using Tor is that it allows you to create hidden services that will mask your identity to other users. In fact, you can have a website that is untraceable to you personally, provided you've taken all security precautions to keep your system updated. Here is an example of an onion site only accessible by using Tor:http://duskgytldkxiuqc6.onion/ Naturally you can't access this with your Firefox browser without Tor. hence the "hidden" name.

This chapter will give you the basics on what you need to set up your own Tor hidden service. It's not meant to be all-inclusive that covers everything and the kitchen sink, but only to give you an idea of the technical know-how you need to possess.Step One: Ensure Tor Works Follow the directions on installing Tor, securing it against exploits and security vulnerabilities first and foremost. Windows directions are here, Linux here, and OS X here. Each OS has

it's own vulnerabilities, with Windows
being the worst. I recommend you go
with Linux after you've mastered the
basics as it gives you more control over
Tor and is far more resistant to attacks
than Windows.Now might be a good time to state
the obvious, something you've probably
realized by now, and that is this: That no
two counter-intelligence experts ever do
the same thing the same way all the time.
There is no red pill that makes it "All
Clear." No cheat sheet of Magic Opsec
Sauce that everyone can master if they
only gulp it down. You can't memorize
every organic compound combination in
Organic Chemistry. Believe me, I tried.
There were far too many.What you do however is memorize
the general principles, from which you
can derive a solution to every problem
that comes about. Anonymity is
sometimes like that. Your strengths will
not be your neighbor's strengths. Your
weaknesses will be different as well.
You adapt as you go along, and I can
guarantee you your skills as a hobbyist
will far exceed those working on the
government dole.
Step Two: Installing Your Own Web
ServerA local web server is the first thing
you need to configure. It is a bit more
involved than space here allows
(without jacking the price) but if you do
not know what a web server is, there is
a simple guide here.
You also want to keep this local
server separate from any other
installations that you have to avoid
cross-contamination. In fact, you don't
want ANY links between your hidden
server and your day-to-day computerusage outside Tor.
Your server must be set to disallow
any data leaks that might give away your
identity. So you must attach the server to
localhost only. If you're swapping trade
secrets and don't want the boss to know,

use a virtual machine to prevent DNS
and other data leaks, but only if you can
access the physical host yourself.
Professional web hosting services (i.e.
the Cloud) are a big no-no since it is
stupid easy for the admin to snatch your
encryption keys from RAM.Go to http://localhost:8080/ via
browser, since that is the port-number
you entered at creation. Copy a text doc
to the usual html-folder and ensure it
copies successfully by logging into the
webpage.Configuration Time
Now comes the part where most
people quit. Don't worry, it isn't hard.
It's just that beginners see these numbers
and think "Oh no... math!" and throw the
book out the window.
But that's not what you'll do...
because you're a smart cookie.First, set your hidden-service to link
to your own web-server. You can use
Notepad to open your "torrc" file within
Tor directory and do a search for the
following piece of code:
########### This section is just for
location-hidden services ###
As you can see, the hidden services
function of Tor is edited out by the "#"
sign, where each row relates to a hidden
service. HiddenServiceDir is the sectionthat will house all data about your own
hidden service. Within this will be the
hostname.file. This is where your onion-
url will be.
The "HiddenServicePort" allows
you to set a decoy port for redirects to
throw off any efforts at detecting you. So
add these to your torrc file.
HiddenServiceDir
/Library/Tor/var/lib/tor/hidden_service/
HiddenServicePort 80
127.0.0.1:8080Next, alter the HiddenServiceDir to
the real directory from which Tor runs.
For Windows, use:
HiddenServiceDir
C:\Users\username\Documents\tor\hidden_
HiddenServicePort 80

127.0.0.1:8080
For Linux:
/home/username/hidden_service/,
substituting "username" with whateveryou named that directory.
Restart Tor after saving the Torrc-
file and it should be operational. Check
your spelling if it throws out any errors.
Now then. Two files are created: the
private_key and the hostname; private
keys for your hidden service which you
should keep under lock and key. The
hostname is not your private key,
however. You can give this to anyone
you wish.A descriptor for the hidden
service links to other Tor servers and
their respective directories so that Tor
users can download it anonymously
when they link or access to your hidden
server.
Other points of note:
- Visitors to your hidden service may
be able to identify whether your web-
server is Thttpd or Apache.
- If your offline 50% of the time, sowill your hidden service. Little bits (or
lengthy ones, in this case) of data like
this are useful to an adversary creating a
profile on you.
- It is wiser to create a hidden
service on Tor clients versus Tor relays
as the relay uptime is visible to the
public.
- Be aware that you are not a Node
by default. On that point, it is advised to
not have a relay running on the same
machine as your hidden service as thisopens security risks.
Shallot and Scallion Option
You also have the option of using
Shallot or Scallion. Shallot allows one
to create a customized .onion address for
a hidden service, such as
yyyyynewbietestyyyy.onionOn Running a Hidden Tor
Server (and other Opsec
Magic Sauce)
Having used Tor for many years, it
came as a pleasant surprise to learn how

few incidents there were in which the
NSA managed to disrupt Tor. And I don't
mean spam, either, but rather something
that brought large sections of the
network to a grinding halt. As it turnsout, they're bark is much worse than their
bite, especially if one is vigilant with
their own secure setup.
The thing is, most Tor users couldn't
be bothered. But then most users aren't
interested in running a hidden server just
as most P2P users don't bother seeding.
Most are hit n' run downloaders. They
know that as U.S. citizens they stand a
good chance of getting sued if they leave
their balls out there long enough. So
some users opt to not further their own
security knowledge. Let the Tor devs doit, they say. Can't be bothered.
Except most of the Tor advice by Tor
developers I've read come up woefully
inadequate. In fact I find that they aren't
paranoid nearly enough. It's always
been my belief that you can never be
sufficiently paranoid as far as protecting
your freedom is concerned, since the
powers that be want to capture it and
bottle it the way a cancer captures
control of a cell: One organelle at a time
with little of it's environment aware of
the slow-boiling attack. To be honest... Isuspect they depend on apathy and
ignorance. And a lot of users gladly
oblige.
Mr. Frog, meet boiling pot of water...
So then, what can we do? Well for
starters, we can get the right security
mindset.
Tor and Your PCA secure computer is your best
defense as the NSA mostly relies on
man-in-the-middle attacks and browser
exploits that deliver payloads to hidden
Tor servers. That said, you should
anticipate and expect such an exploit
can infiltrate your system at any point.
Things like Nits (network bugs), you
have to be aware of. Thus the need to
adhere to the following:

- Use Linux whenever possible. Yes,
I know you're comfortable using
Windows and think Linux too much of abother. But you won't if you're ISP is
subpoenaed for something you said on
Facebook. Something anti-feminist, for
instance. So learn to use it.
As you can see in these NSA slides -
they typically target the weakest system.
The Tor Browser Bundle for Windows
was instrumental in taking down
Freedom Hosting and Silk Road because
of unpatched vulnerabilities. That, and a
few rogue Tor exit nodes patched
unsigned Windows packages to spread
malware.If you're new to Linux, look at Linux
Mint. If you're experienced, Debian is a
good choice. Windows can't be trusted
primarily because it is closed-source,
but also because malware is more
effective on it than Linux. If Linux is out
of the question, consider Tails or
Whonix as these apps come
preconfigured to not allow any outgoing
connections to clearnet.
Update Update Update!Your PC must also be updated,
always. Not updating leads to
vulnerabilities and exploits such as
those in Windows. Optimally, you
should ensure Tails is always updated
each time you use Tor, and avoid any
sites that use Java/Javascript/Flash or
any kind of scripting as these execute
code in ways you cannot see. Use these
only in an emergency and never in your
home system.
Avoid using cookies wherever
possible. Consider installing the Self-Destructing Cookies add-on.
Again, you should not use anything
but a portable PC since your home PC is
most likely not portable enough to be
discarded in a trash can in the event of
compromise.
Avoid Google like the Black Plague.
Use DuckDuckGo or Startpage instead
for your Tor sessions.

Situation AwarenessHere we go again, preachin' the same old song and dance. But reading things three times often becomes a trigger in the brain later on for taking action, so here it is. Again.

If an agency can monitor your local connection as well as the link you are browsing, then (with sufficient resources) they can apply traffic analysis to pinpoint your real location. Therefore, I recommend you do not use Tor in your residence.Just to clarify, do not use Tor in your legal residence if doing any kind of covert work or anything illegal without strict security measures in place; the kind the average Tor user will likely overlook. Let that other guy learn his lesson. It's a tough break, but better him than you. He's a 19 year old named Jimmy who likes hacking. You're a 32 year old construction guy with two kids and a mortgage. Who has more to lose? Right, you. So study counter-surveillance and counter-forensics likeyour life depends on it... because it does!

For enemies of the state-level operations, I would suggest not engaging anything even near your online PC at home. Certainly nothing that makes you think you need Tor to hide it. It may be fine for private browsing but not for someone planning a coup, running an illegal operation (home bible study in Iran, for instance), or trying to disappear.Be wary of using it in hotels as well, where often there are many cams watching with 24/hr surveillance. That location can be linked to Tor activity.

Do not use Tor more than a day in any specific location. A correlation-attack can be done in less than an hour if a black van is parked nearby--a van you will not see. They may not slap the cuffs on you as you walk out of the cafe that very week, but later they might.

Consider the area a toxic dump after a
day, regardless if you must travel to thenext shop or town.
If you want to get really cloak and
dagger about it, have an app running (an
MMO, for instance) while you are out
and about doing your Tor activity that
makes it look like you were home during
that time.
"We've been watching you Mr.
Anderson, and it seems you've been
living... two... lives." -- Agent Smith,The MatrixDarknet Personas
You've no doubt read of Tor busts
where an undercover agent snagged a
phone number or clearnet nic from
someone they were targeting because
said target trusted too much, too quickly.You can avoid this by retraining
yourself, unlearning what you've
learned.
You must consider your Tor sessions
the property of your other Self. The
cloned You - that shadowy thievish
looking guy above. The second You. One
that despises Incubus and loves Tool and
views Neo as just another beta-orbiting
punk who got the luck of the draw when
Morpheus and crew unplugged him. This
clone would not use Twitter or YouTube
or other social gunk. He would neverhang with you nor call you up for a few
beers. In fact, he hates beer, preferring
J&B as he hacks with John Carpenter's
The Thing OST playing as mood music
in the background. That's your other You.
The smarter you.
And he must be the new You on Tor.
And you must forever separate him from
the non-Tor You.
His Facebook, Twitter and YouTube
accounts are all fake, having never once
used them on his home PC. His nics aredifferent, as is his passwords,
likes/dislikes and even the fonts he uses
to browse the Deep Web. Mixing this
dark persona with your own would be
like the boy made of matter kissing the
anti-matter girl...
BOOM.

Further, any phone calls this person makes is done by prepaid phones that were not purchased by any credit cards he holds. He is a cash n' carry guy and then only if he is twenty miles fromhome. Any SIM cards he uses are strictly used in conjunction with Tor activity and never used in phones the other guy uses. And... he deliberately leaves false info wherever he goes. Kinda like the CIA does.

But to better clarify this idea, let's assume John Doe doesn't know any better. He watches a movie on Netflix. Then he mosies on over to Freenet and drops intel without even realizing it, eager to share his great cinema experience with his darknet buds (nopun). "Hey guys, just watched a cool flick with Russell Crowe. Kinda Michael Bay-ish and Liam Neeson's cameo was too short, but makes for a good flick if you want to learn how to disappear. But those police, sweet Jesus! Those rent-a-cop guys sure are as dumb as a sack of bricks!"

Police are dumb, he says. Metadata is collected by Netflix justas it is with Google and Yahoo. Every single user. They know every film you viewed and even which ones you hated. He's even made forum posts indicating similar weather and, though not mentioning names, has griped about local politicians being handcuffed in very geo-specific arrests, even dropping the charges!

How many Netflix fans do you think watched this movie at the time of his Freenet post? How many in cities that had local politicians arrested forembezzling? How many with similar weather depicted in the film? Most likely less than ten. Maybe not even that.

There is also the handwriting element. Does he mispell the same words over and over? Throw commas like daggers? Misuse semi-colons and

run-on sentences? System clock out of
sync with his posts? All of this leads to
a great profile that ties his IP address to
his identity. Often it is enough to get a
warrant if he so much as whispers that
he's obtained any kind of contraband.Unless of course, all of this info is
tailor-made to fit the other You.
We already know that the VPN
called Hide-My-Ass as well as
Hushmail and Lavabit stabbed their
users in the back when threats by a judge
became too heated ($5000 a day in
Lavabit's case, until they forked over
user data). And all this just so they could
track Edward Snowden.
Bottom line: Learn from Snowden'smistakes. Take every company's claim of
anonymity with a grain of salt. The proof
is in the amount of arrests tied to said
company or app. In the case of Freenet...
none.
But there is always a first time.
Recall that they only have to get lucky
once, which more often than not relies
on your carelessness.Tor Hidden Services - High Risk, High
Reward
CNN along with FoxNews has been
trumpeting the defeat of certain hidden
services for a few years now. Services
like Silk Road and Freedom Hosting,
which I'm sure you've heard about. They
are a easy target for the FBI since hidden
services are not high on the list of
priorities by Tor developers yet. Same
for the NSA.Both agencies know every trick and
hack there is to know about running a
hidden service. And so should you. This
is not to say you need the expertise to
match their team of super hackers, but
that you need even more vigilance to run
such a service than you do visiting such
a service.
Priority number one is simple: if you
run one, you must own one. They must
not be run under somebody else's control
if you can help it, because if that service

is compromised, everyone goes down. That means total anonymity, 100% of the time with world-class jewel-thief stealth ability.

The Silk Road admin did not have this ability. In fact, looking through the online docs detailing the arrest, one gets the impression he was very lax in IT security procedure. He repeatedly made mistakes such that luck on the part of LE never really came into it at all. The guy was just sloppy.

FirstNever, ever, ever run a hidden service within a VM that is owned by a friend or a Cloud space provider. Remember, all "The Cloud" is, is someone else's drive or network, not your own. Encryption keys can be dumped from RAM. And who owns the RAM?

Right. The Cloud provider. Lightning strikes and there goes your own anonymity as well as the anonymity of your visitors if they are lazy in theirbrowser habits. The FBI delivered a "nit" (network investigative technique) this way to unpatched Tor Browser Bundles in 2013. If, however, you own the machine, then it's a different story. But let's back up a few steps and assume you don't. How might you go about running it on a host system?

Well first off, you would need two separate physical hosts from different parties, both running in virtual machines with a firewall-enabled OS that only allows Tor network activity and nothingelse. The second physical host is the one the hidden service runs from, also VM'ed. Secure connections are enabled by IPSec. What's IPSec, you ask?

"IPSec is a protocol suite, for securing Internet Protocol (IP) communications by authenticating and encrypting each IP packet of a communication session. IPsec can be used in protecting data flows between a

pair of hosts (host-to-host), between a pair of security gateways (network-to-network), or between a security gateway and a host (network-to-host)."
If an intruder agent tampers with anything, you will know about it and can shut down the service or move it to a safer place, and all while being a ghost in the machine. You can imagine how valuable this would be in North Korea. If you were in that cesspool of a country, you would be more than a little paranoid if the server went down even for a few seconds. But you could always move it to a more secure location or even start over, and you might just want to since you would not know if a RAID failure had occurred or if some commie jackboot was sending a copy of the VM to the higher ups.
Second
If going the host route, you must ensure that remote-console is always available to you by the host, any time you want. You must do everything remotely, in fact, and change passwords frequently via https. I'd say once per day as paranoia in such a climate as North Korea would be good for your health.
Third
You must never, not even once, access the service from home. Not from your Nexus 7. Not from your girlfriend's Galaxy Note. Not even via Tor from your backyard using your neighbor's WiFi. Using a VPN as well is risky unless you know what you're doing. Only access it via secure locations at least ten miles away from your residence. Overkill, some might say, but then there is no such thing as overkill in a gulag.
Fourth
Move the service on occasion. Again, look at any Youtube video on how snipers train to take out an enemy. They move place to place after each shot to conceal the true location from the enemy. How often is up to you. Once a week? Once a month? Personally I'd say every twenty-one days. You can never be

too secure when running one of these.The Death of Anonymity
Prime minister David Cameron went
on record in January, 2015 to say he
wanted to outlaw all encryption-enabled
messaging apps if the government cannot
have backdoor keys to decrypt
encryption. It is beyond preposterous. It
would be like a farmer allowing easy
entry to the henhouse to cougars as well
as foxes. While on the campaign trail, he
said:"Are we going to allow a means of
communications which it simply isn't
possible to read? My answer to that
question is: No, we must not."
While he referred to mostly chat
programs like WhatsApp and what not,
you can bet the ranch he was also talking
about apps like PGP, Freenet and the
discontinued Truecrypt. Regrettably, he
used the Hebdo (cartoonist) attack as
justification (don't they all use these to
further Big Brother agendas?).I see a similar trend evolving in
Canada regarding VPN usage. New laws
now require VPNs to identify customers
who download copyrighted works like
movies and games so that infringement
notices (i.e. scare letters) get to the right
person. That sounds rather just on the
surface of it, because who wouldn't deny
George Lucas's ability to make more
Star Wars prequels? Art, you know.
But therein is the problem. Mainly
it's that politicians forget how the
internet actually works.Doing what they dictate means VPN
providers must retain access logs for 6
months, minimum. This alone pretty
much guarantees a VPN's ability to sell
anonymity services (privacy, actually)
will dissolve, thus leading to massive
losses as customers aren't stupid. They
know when their privacy is being
targeted. Let the exodus begin!
(Government cookie parties)
They also know that VPNs assign
shared IP addresses for customers. One

might be yourself, there in your jammiessipping Rickard's Red while downloading the latest NiN video
YouTube seemingly blocked, while the other user is Uncle Frick downloading something from the Usenet group guys-who-like-bouncing-pigtailed-girls-on-a-knee.

The only solution is to move out of Canada altogether.

But then, perhaps that is what the government wanted all along.The saddest part isn't that none of this won't stop terrorism or copyright infringement, or that it will hurt most private encryption vendor's businesses or that only politicians will have encryption while the citizens have none. No, the saddest part is that we will have become the frog-in-the-pot who turns the oven on ourselves to maximum temperature and then slip back into the pot, and all because someone more powerful than you or I said it was the right thing to do.Our world will become Bizarro World. Where right is wrong and light is dark and no one has security except for the agents of the new Matrix they will build. Where to be more secure is to be less secure as us peons go... because if the government says so, well, that must be the gospel truth because when's the last time a politician lied?

If you learn nothing else, remember two things: Backdoors are security holes in 100% of cases. The second one is like it: Anonymity and Privacy and thefreedom that comes of it will only die if we let it.Closing Thoughts

As you can see, the powers that be are actively targeting your ability to make choices about your own freedom. They work in baby steps. They think you're stupid. They think they can run your life better than you can. Only they can't. Did the NSA stop the attack on Charlie Hebdo, the French cartoonist? Did they stop 9/11? The bombings in

Spain? A death from a thousand cuts, a
little at a time, and before you know ityou're feeling very light-headed but
aren't quite sure why.
Believe me, putting off your security
and peace of mind will be enough to fuel
that tsunami of cancer they're building up
one cell at a time. If you've read this
book then you've already taken all the
baby steps you need. You've dipped your
big toe into that whirlpool and it's high
time you jumped in. Don't procrastinate.
You know how warm the water is. Wait
too long and the water might get too
cold. Worse still is that someone mightjust lock you out altogether.
Just remember: Always nourish a
strong security mindset. Develop an
ability to configure things logically and
anticipate trouble way ahead of time,
seeing weaknesses in your submarine
before the water comes roaring in. If in
doubt about this, watch the film 'The
Abyss'. See how Bud reacts when the
water comes roaring in? He panics!
Most of the crew dies. Don't wait till
that fateful day. Have something set up
long ahead of time. A plan B. A plan C.Even a plan D if you can afford it.
Any intelligence agency has
unlimited funding to kill freedom by
censoring all of us - even censoring the
freedom to buy what you want to buy.
With the media in their back pocket they
can conjure any boogeyman they want to
run over you. It's not illegal for them to
lie to you, but it is for you to lie to them.
This hypocrisy costs them nothing but
costs you everything, so like them, you
must keep on top of changes to good
security, updating as necessary and beingon constant alert of new zero-day
threats.
But if there is one thing that you have
that they don't, it's the incentive to work
harder than they do. They clock out at
5pm every day. Will you? The powers
that be play dirty. And so should you.Want to Know More?
First off, I owe you a big thanks and

a round of beer for downloading this
book. You could have picked any one of
dozens of great books on this topic. You
took a chance with mine. So thank you
for that. Seriously, reading to the end
takes a strong mind. If you liked what
you read then I need your help! Please
take a moment to leave a review for this
book on Amazon so others can learn touse Tor and Freenet and, well, protect
themselves.
Speaking of protection, I've used a
number of tools to get to where I'm at,
and some of the topics that failed to pass
the censors in this book quite
miraculously managed to slip through in
my other books. Go figure.
One thing though: when you have not
one but two or three silver bullets to
take down a werewolf, the better your
chances of staying invisible to any otherlycans roaming around out there. Mind
you, I'm not prejudiced against those
with Lycanthropy, as it is no laughing
matter. But then neither is herd mentality.
So then. Don't use the same tools
everyone else is using all the time. Mix
it up a bit by checking out some other
stuff of mine that did not see the light of
day in this release:
More Kindle eBooks by Lance
Darknet: A Guide to StayingAnonymous Online (Audio & Kindle)
Usenet and the Future of Anonymity
How to Be Invisible Offline and On:
Disappear Without a Trace!
Anonymous File Sharing: How to Be
a Ghost in the Machine
Social Media in an Anti-Social
World
Tor and the Dark Art of Anonymity
Freenet: The Ultimate Deep Web
Portal.

Best regards,
your friend and Author Raffaele De Rosa